GET OVER BEING humiliated

# Advance Praise

"Leesa is an amazing writer who overcame diversity and tells her story from a real perspective. Leesa lived everything she tells her readers.

If there was ever a true formula to returning to a normal and productive life, this is it. Leesa was able to take a very real issue, hitting rock bottom, only to turn around and deliver a very positive direction and path to purpose.

If you are looking for a book to help with self-esteem and how to deal with regret, *Get Over Being Humiliated* is it. I like the way her story is explained in simple terms with a practical plan of action.

The presentation of the steps to live beyond regrets are fantastic. This is an amazing book, highly recommended for anyone who wrestles with guilt, how to figure out others and/or themselves, or is starting over.

I think this book is a must-read for everyone and I highly recommend it."

**—Larry Mekus,**
Real Estate Broker

"I have been a sister-in-law to Leesa for forty-five years. She was always a little bitty thing with a big heart and an even bigger laugh, but what I really see in her now is her amazing strength.

Tumbling from the pinnacle of success to the depths of despair, she was able to pick herself up and see her misfortune in a positive light—as a way to help others—even with a five-pound lock box around her ankle. If I could use just one word to describe her it would be authentic. She is the real deal."

—**Agnes Santomenno,** Owner,
Reprosa Panama Jewelry and Columbian Artifacts

"I am the oldest of Leesa's three children. I struggle more than most, but I love my mom and I know she loves me, and this is her story. It's not about me, it's not about her. It's about how regardless of your hardships or circumstances, you can endure and move past and through heartache, troubles and things you never thought you could live through. It's the rainbow at the end of the storm.

She has never been one to sweep anything under the rug—never let me get away with that. So, here she is now, wanting to help you or anyone who has gone through the most devastating, challenging time of your life. She definitely knows how to pick herself up and loves showing others how as well. That is her passion.

She has a sincere love for people. I know you will get so much out of reading this book. It will help you get over anything that is keeping you stuck in pain, embarrassment, or any other obstacle that convinces you that this is as good as it gets."

**—Taylor Wehrli**

"Well, really what can I say? I met Leesa a few years back and as you know, in the real estate business you meet many people from around the world, different personalities, different traditions and cultures. She is, for a southern word, a 'hoot,' but a very smart, sensitive, truly caring person who will take a breath and listen to you when you are expressing yourself in business or personally. She never judges and is an all-around very sweet and caring person who has had many trials in life, but they have made her strong, understanding, and appreciative of every day in life. As most of us know, there is something in our lives that usually 'makes us or breaks us,' and thankfully, it has made Leesa into the beautiful soul she is. May reading her book bring 'POWER' to everyone because we ALL deserve a peaceful and strong journey through life."

**—Donna Knowles,**
VIP Real Estate, Columbus, GA

"I love...love...loved this book! I do have to admit that upon reading the title of the book, I thought, 'another self-help read,' but instead, I was truly inspired and connected with the author's emotions. Overwhelming fear, rejection, shame, and humiliation are conquered with love, faith, self-respect and a willingness to continue life's wonderful journey only to discover the true meaning and purpose as to why we are here. It is to leave a traceable, everlasting imprint and renewed emotion, along with healing and gratitude. The author's rawness and vulnerability provide the reader with the desire to emerge from the darkness and into the light with renewed optimism and hope. Self-forgiveness allows us to push past the highest peak with relentless force and emerge into a valley of restored purpose, empowerment, humility and a profusion of self-worth and love."

**—Estela Williamson,**
Prolific Real Estate, San Diego, CA

"I finally understand the depth of hardship my mother endured, and more so, how her persistence lead to strength in such trying times. *Get Over Being Humiliated* is an epic torn between her battle with the grips of shame and chagrin, and the renewing power of family and relentless ambition."

**—Thomas Ward,**
L.A. County Firefighter

"I knew Leesa when she owned and operated her successful real estate company. I worked with and for her for many years. Regardless of title, degree or status, she is the same loving person…still always wanting to give.

This is a story and account of rise and fall, success and failure, depression, rut, loss of her entire existence and how she rose again. Guaranteed, she can definitely help you."

**—Phillip Snelling,** Owner,
Advanced Carpet Cleaning, Tracy, CA

"When Leesa told me about her book, *Get Over Being Humiliated* I was intrigued, so I started reading, and could not stop. It is a powerful biography describing the contrast from being at the top to eventually falling, and even enduring lawsuits by clients.

This is a blueprint for change and creating a better life. I love her resilience as a strong businesswoman and admire her courage."

**—Aileen D'Andrea,**
Retired Paralegal

"When Leesa says in her book that she cares about you as her reader, she really does!

I 'met' Leesa through various Facebook group posts while working on our books. We could tell from the start that we were kindred souls. We eventually sent some private Facebook messages back and forth to encourage and support each other through our book writing process. She really did understand what I was going through. I wondered if she would be 'the real deal' when we met in person. Wow! It was like we had been friends for life. Her love, compassion, care and sensitivity, wisdom and great sense of humor came pouring out. She really did 'get' me and my life situation and loves me like a sister. Leesa really does 'get' you and your life situation, loves you like a sister or brother, and wants to help you get over humiliation."

—**Rita Pampel,** Author,
*A Parent's Care: Creating a Loving Balance for Family & Aging Parents*

"Reading this book by Leesa will inspire you in many ways. Not only will it help you rise from the depths of the humiliation of losing a business, but it will communicate to you the way to come back from any of life's personal humiliations. If you have been one of the lucky ones who has never had to experience such a thing, this book will warm your soul through the love, passion and inner soul-searching that Leesa reveals. Leesa, you have a great story and I wish you the happiest final chapter in your life."

—**M. Camero,**
Postal Annex Owner, Glendora, CA

"I've been reading this book all day. I've cried several times. I can relate so much. What comes to mind is Isaiah 61:3 'HE gives us beauty for ashes.' You have overcome so much I'm sure you are a stronger person because of it. Thank you so much for sharing your story. From California to Georgia your story gives others hope. I'm looking forward to meeting you in person soon. God bless you!"

**—Becky Ann Wright,**
Medical Technologist

"I loved how open and raw Leesa was. It made me feel like I'm not alone. Totally relatable regardless of your circumstances. Painstaking accounts of past, devastation, regret and bringing yourself back up again to start over and live the life you were meant and designed, and deserve to live."

**—Maria Mekus,** Partner/Owner to
Prolific Real Estate, San Diego, CA

"Heart-filled and expressing what most of us are too afraid to admit or face. Leesa provides an invitation to be real and unapologetically authentic, allowing real healing through experiences, self-reflection and bravery, to move past the past. Willing to expose the deepest part of her own shame in order to connect with the reader on a sincere level, offering guidance and solutions for the silent pain of humiliation."

**—Jonathan Steinberg,**
Retired Broker

"*Get Over Being Humiliated* is fantastic! In clear writing Leesa Ward lets her readers know how awful her life has been, but she survived. She did it her way—the way of a strong and wise woman. *Get Over Being Humiliated* is so clear to understand and so full of lessons for all of us."

**—Elizabeth Kroft,**
Costa Rica Business Owner

"*Rising Star-Crash Landing* was the front-page cover of the Tracy Press, CA, November 2006. This book is an account of a once-successful real estate broker/owner, who fell hard with depression, was broken, and lost hope for years, but rose up again to prove, All Things Are Possible…if you believe. After reading this book, You Will Believe."

**—Erica Hall,** Realtor,
Klemm Real Estate, Tracy, CA

# GET OVER BEING humiliated

## How to Conquer the World
## Even If You Feel Rejected

# LEESA WARD

NEW YORK

LONDON • NASHVILLE • MELBOURNE • VANCOUVER

# Get Over Being Humiliated

## How to Conquer the World Even if You Feel Rejected

Published in New York, New York, by Morgan James Publishing in partnership with Difference Press. Morgan James is a trademark of Morgan James, LLC. www.MorganJamesPublishing.com

ISBN 9781631951220 paperback
ISBN 9781631951237 eBook
Library of Congress Control Number: 2020935455

**Cover Design by:**
Megan Dillon
megan@creativeninjadesigns.com

**Interior Design by:**
Christopher Kirk
www.GFSstudio.com

**Editor:**
Emily Tuttle

**Book Coaching:**
The Author Incubator

New International Version
The Holy Bible, New International Version', NIV'. Copyright © 1973, 1978, 1984, 2011 by Biblica, Inc.™ Used by Permission. All rights reserved worldwide.

New King James Version
Scripture taken from the New King James Version®. Copyright © 1982 by Thomas Nelson, Inc. Used by permission. All rights reserved.

Morgan James is a proud partner of Habitat for Humanity Peninsula and Greater Williamsburg. Partners in building since 2006.

Get involved today! Visit
MorganJamesPublishing.com/giving-back

*I dedicate this book especially to you… you, who picked it up and who are holding it right now, and to anyone else who's ever felt lost, alone, devastated, and filled with shame and humiliation. To those who do not know what to do, just need a fresh start, and someone there to help.*

# Table of Contents

# Chapter 1:

# You Are Here— The Starting Point

You are and have been your own worst enemy - judgmental, condemning, and torturing yourself beyond what's necessary, beyond the "conviction," beyond time due for the "crimes" you've committed, for the hurt you've implemented or contributed to, flooded with regret (oh my goodness, the regret) and the feeling of not being worthy of any kind of happiness or joy in response. Guilt, quickly on cue, slaps you hard in the face just in case you might have forgotten all the mistakes you've made. It's your not-so-friendly reminder of how so many others have been affected by your actions or what has transpired... so many lives, families, businesses, and relationships, leaving you paralyzed with the weight of liability, disgrace, and fault.

So here you are, frozen in pause and unable to press play. I know exactly how you feel. And I know for a fact it's an extremely lonely journey, one that isn't necessarily at the forefront of others' minds, and yet overwhelms yours - obliterating any chance to escape from memory. It's hard to imagine what that feels like, until you experience the true depths of all that you've lost and what that represents, what it means, and how every little thing, affects every other little thing that equals the entirety of your life. It's the butterfly effect, that seems to trickle control and suffocate you in shame. I was there, drowning in the same darkness, hiding in the shadows, wanting to be invisible - just waiting... for "it" to somehow feel or be different. It somehow makes us feel a little better knowing somebody else comprehends and understands the pain and what you're dealing with and that, yes, there is a solution and it can lead the way to a proven path.

I will show you the step- by- step roadmap of how to achieve relief from guilt, humiliation, and pain and provide the techniques to help get you through the obstructions that keep you stuck, releasing you from the recurring circumstances that keep you where you are. I'm going to show how it is possible, and maybe even a blessing, for you to create a new life - a life designed with purpose, one you will want to wake up for with wide eyes and gleaming desire, triggered with the irresistible motive to finally start living again. I'm going to share with you how you can move past your past, providing you with my own personal experiences and resources, tips, and strategies to help you finally heal, and ultimately regain control of the steering wheel that seems to have to jerked you across the centerline and into oncoming traffic.

This is the hardest part: commitment to finally do something. It's the hardest part to decide, to risk stepping out of your comfort zone, trusting there is something else beyond the "this" you're existing in. You can move beyond the fear and make the decision to start fresh, knowing all things are possible and that you can achieve all that you want. It's not over. You're not over. It's only the beginning − your new beginning to create and live life even more than you ever imagined. You'll finally shed your insecurity and develop your new strengths of unstoppable endurance. You will see how the seemingly insignificant actions you take daily, based on the steps I provide, will completely turn your life around and finally stop the reruns of your old story and allow your new script to be written.

When will you finally let yourself feel deserving to take out the key that you've had in your pocket this whole time and unlock the prison door - releasing yourself from the shackles of your past that have enslaved your life for far too long? Let's choose **now**. Welcome to your new life and fresh start! I'm excited for you.

## Bad News: It's Rock Bottom

But the good news is that it's the perfect foundation for building your new life - the starting point to assess where you are and where you want to go.

There wasn't any kind of book like this when I was feeling lost and alone, not knowing where to turn or what to do. I felt humiliation and shame and tried to figure out what I could do to turn everything around and start over fresh. What do you do, and where do you even begin, when the only life you knew and loved is gone? When you are no longer who you used to be? It seems as if life slows down to allow all the shame to continue to wash over you, saturating your every pore, leaving you feeling powerless under the weight that binds you.

My story is going to be different from yours, but I can assure you we share the same devastation regardless of the level of circumstance or reason. It's the same heartache and loneliness that most couldn't even comprehend unless they've gone through something similar. I'm not sure what exactly put you in the position of leaving your job and feeling shame, embarrassment, guilt, total humiliation, or anything else that makes you feel worthless and like giving up, but I do know everybody has a story - heartache, past circumstances, and tragedies of all levels that can leave you feeling like the world has just fallen apart. Yes, for you it has. Nothing will ever be the same, and you can't ever imagine anything other than this current nightmare and disaster.

Trust me, I get it. It has taken me a long time, way too long, to overcome and move past it all, as well as believe that everything I went through was for a reason and a purpose - definitely not something I even entertained for years without anger and resistance. Not kidding! I gave up over thirteen years of my life trying to dig myself out of the pit of depression, feeling like a total failure and being in limbo with complete uncertainty about any and everything. It resulted in me basically just existing, dreading every day and hoping I would somehow feel and be different the next. It was literally the scariest time and the loneliest I have ever felt. Feeling hopeless was all I knew, and it utterly consumed me. It's so much more than just losing a career. There are so many repercussions mentally, emotionally, and physically that come with it. Your identity, self-esteem, value, worth, security and pride in the life that you worked so hard to build, all at question or even obliterated - a life you never imagined would be different than what it was. And now, here you are, forced to try and start all over when you feel less than living; seemingly an impossible feat. Again, I know this all too well. It's the hardest and worst thing you've ever gone through. So how do you get over it? Over this..?

## This is for Reason

If you've picked up this book, it's for a reason. Whatever your story is compared to mine, it doesn't matter. It's not a competition of whose story is worse. It's the same and equal when it comes to hurting and being at the lowest point of your life. And I've got to believe there is a reason and purpose - there's got to be. It's how the universe works. Even though it scares me to death to expose myself for all the world to see and once again be judged, I feel the need and am finally brave enough to share my experience. How can you not? I feel a responsibility to help anyone else going through a similar situation dealing with pain and shame and devastation, keeping you stuck on this merry-go-round of misery and uncertainty and leaving you feeling like you're living a life with no genuine meaning or purpose. It's also the reason I wanted to write this book for you so that you don't have to waste over a decade, stumbling around, losing relationships and credibility like I did... basically losing your life little by little, slowly but surely.

## A Journal Entry from Me - February 20th, 2015 7:48 a.m.

*Dear Ree, as I sit on my fuchsia bean bag, going through the pile of papers, pictures, notes and magazine clippings I can't seem to throw away, I came across two beautiful cards you sent me last year January 13th, 2014 and February 8th. (Do you always date your cards and letters?) That is something I taught Baelee and Thomas from the moment they could pick up a crayon to draw, telling them that they need to capture and remember this moment forever. I even got Baelee in the habit of stamping it with the time, knowing that everything is designed and happens for a reason and it's nice to look back and trace the events that led up to a moment, putting the pieces of the puzzle together to reveal the message God sends and speaks to us through. It helps to confirm, with confidence, that there is no such thing as coincidence... not in the way the majority of the world considers it.*

*If our eyes are open, we can see. If we are quiet, we can hear. There are so many gifts around us just waiting to be opened. Do we take the time or quickly walk by, rushing on to what we believe is worthy of our attention? We're always in pursuit, searching and seeking, when all along, it's right in front of us. It's in everything... the flowers, beautiful in design, drenched with color from the most delicate pastel, to the vibrant burst of deep purple and red's...my favorite.*

I've always told my kids from a very young age that we're lucky and blessed when we are able to look at others' mistakes or worse circumstances to learn from, instead of having to go through the pain ourselves. Regardless, compassion and empathy are so important. It's so easy to judge others when you haven't walked in their shoes. I have learned so much from being in the position that I am and that I was in. I've noticed that it isn't until we're able to look back after going and coming through something that we really appreciate and see the whole light and truth of what happened.

## Take My Hands

It is my most heartfelt desire to be with you through this time of uncertainty. I truly wish that I had somebody, some advice and direction, or some place to go that could have helped me without wasting over a decade of my life trying to get over it myself. Seriously, I have read hundreds of books over the years about love, healing, spiritual intuition, law of attraction, psychology, forgiveness - every kind of self-help, motivation and the like - and I was still unable to pick myself up after my devastating circumstance/ life changing "event"/ turn of the corner/ mid-life crisis... whatever you want to call it. There was nothing like this when I was going through it, and I felt I was the only one. And even if I wasn't, nobody was talking about it; nobody ever wants to admit anything other than "Business is great!" and "Life is wonderful."

This is my hope for you with this book: it's a sincere love letter to you, wanting so much to help you out of something I *know* so well, to give you hope by knowing life *can* be different, and I'm here to help. I have my arms stretched out for you. Take my hands, and I'll hold yours tight. I want to pull you through this dark uncertainty, this fearful unknown, and show you there is another way. Don't give up or just settle for where you're at right now. You're worth more than who you used to be, worth more than the memories of how it was.

There's so much to my story and I will include everything I think would be helpful for you to know in order to show you how you, too, can heal and move past your current situation; however this book is written not for me and "my" story, but specifically for you - filled with love, understanding, and compassion.

Chapter 2:

# My Story

There are several things I am and have been passionate about, but it all boils down to one goal, one mission: empowering others to be the best they can be with love, acceptance, faith, and self-worth. I believe when you are your best self, confident and full of light, you allow yourself to be vulnerable and open to others, without a front or façade, and thereby truly reaching the human connection. Just by being present and authentically engaged, you make others feel important and that they matter. I sincerely love people. I love knowing and feeling that we are all the same. We're one - wanting approval, acceptance, and unconditional love regardless of all of our flaws and imperfections. It hurts me to see us all suffering in silence, alone, when we can support each other instead. I have such a heart for hurting people. I'm a one-hundred percent empath for everything living - plants, animals, and nature included.

You can literally make a difference with a simple smile. It seriously doesn't take much to make someone feel good. I love being a part of that, knowing that I made an impact even if it is only the tiniest speck of one, a small act of kindness that changes their day. It could be just one thing spoken, verbally or nonverbally, that may have altered the way they saw something or the way they saw themselves. It's always obvious, like a bright light shining down a dark hallway. All of a sudden, they wake up and there is a new life glowing from within. There really is love all around, and when you open up and live in *that* reality, it can't help but be spread to others, near or far, like a contagious virus.

## Using Real Estate as My Vehicle

I felt that I did make that impact, that difference, through owning and operating my real estate company, which gave me the opportunity to provide a positive footprint on a daily basis with my agents, staff, and clients. Music and laughter were a standard practice. My business was the vehicle I was able to accomplish all of this with.

However, at the very top of my game around 2006, I suffered from a nervous breakdown dealing with a son with special needs, diagnosed with RAD (Reactive Attachment Disorder) and having to enroll him out of state in a residential treatment facility specializing in his disorder. If you are unfamiliar with it, it's basically when a person is emotionally unable to connect or trust another, thereby always needing to be in control and will manipulate and do anything to ensure it. They are superficially charming and engaging with strangers and are often able to fool even the most sophisticated and intelligent people, including doctors and therapists, who have not done thorough research on it or understand all it entails. Gone left untreated has resulted in the following famous people with RAD: Ted Bundy, Hitler, Saddam Hussein, Scott Peterson, just to name a few. For more information, you can read it in Nancy Thomas's book or watch the HBO movie "A Child of Rage", the true story of her own daughter. At Taylor's age, now 13, I found myself now having to travel to learn, understand and bond with a son I was afraid of and didn't even trust with my other 2 children. Some nights, I couldn't even sleep out of fear of what may happen to me or the kids. I often worried and wouldn't have put it past him, to stab me over and over in the middle of the night- not that he hated me but that he needed to control the situation and didn't know how to handle it. It was years before I could actually take a shower without hearing (real or not) screaming and imagining what was going on in my absence. Even when he was 2600 miles away. Setting our deck on fire and shooting a BB gun at Thomas one morning before school, was the last straw. Until then, I kept questioning myself, wondering if I was just overreacting or if it was all really that bad. Again, feeling guilty about what I was thinking of my very own son. I had 24 employees and real estate agents, multiple properties, a construction crew and my own clients I worked with, as well as taking care of my elderly mom. I handled it well-for a little while. People used to ask me how I did it, to which I'd say, "what you mean?" To me, it was just what I had to do. I didn't have time to stop and think about it. I just did what needed to be done. After a weekend workshop and meeting with Nancy Thomas, I knew what I had to do. I enrolled Taylor in Chaddock and felt very grateful since their usual cut off age was 12. I did this all with the pressure of trying to keep it together without anyone noticing that I was actually falling apart. After all, I was the rock, a leader, and everyone depended on me; but it seemed like all of a sudden I went from a confident female Tony Robbins, to a scared little girl barely able to get out of bed and face anything.

At the same time, my eighty-one-year-old mom who I was caring for, was suffering from Alzheimer's, and I also had two other children that I needed to be strong for. I am the mother, the adult, the one who's supposed to make them feel safe and secure. How was I supposed to do that and pull it off when *I* was so afraid?

The grand finale of events took place after my breakdown and with my sister Athena taking over the company in hopes to handle everything while I was recovering. This is a sister I would have done anything for, I would have died for. It took eight years of her working with me, for me to even feel comfortable and trust her enough to be able to handle everything and all the responsibility it involved.

I lost everything, my business, houses, reputation...everything I worked so hard for over the last twenty years. But even more devastating, I lost the sense of who I was - my identity, worth, the reason I drew breath every day. I easily worked sixteen to eighteen hours a day, full of energy, loving every minute. There was nothing I'd rather do instead. It was my passion, purpose, and felt was my true life's work. It *was my life,* period.

## Ward 2005 Interview

The following is from an interview in December 2005, which includes a lot of background details that will bring you up to speed of who I was before everything fell apart, when I was top of my game and everybody loved me. It was actually a real honor because it was my peers, my competition, who nominated me to become the agent broker of the month. The publication went out to all real estate agents and brokerage companies throughout the San Joaquin County and Bay Area. Yeah, it helped with credibility and recognition. Being able to position yourself with public evidence and documentation is priceless. It definitely helps when you're on top, but it's actually so much worse when you're not. The negative news can literally destroy you. It seems like that is always what is remembered regardless of all the good things you said and have done in the past. It's gone and forgotten, as if everything else you ever did never existed.

I guess that's just human nature. I understand. It's what makes the gossip celebrity magazines so popular and why people watch the news even though it's manipulating and utilizes the negative to bring in the views, ratings, and steer opinions. Zoning in on learning about someone else's misfortune or failure makes us feel better about ourselves. Suddenly, our life doesn't seem all that bad. "Jeez, I never did that, Bob from Wisconsin."

Back in 2005 though, I seriously didn't feel entitled or worthy of an interview about how awesome my

company and I were, but my personal assistant sched-
uled it anyway. I am far from what may seem or be
portrayed as "religious" based on the publication. Like
everything in life, it's constantly evolving and not so
black and white as I've discovered. We are presented
with so much more than we could even imagine at
times. But this is what it was in 2005 before my crash.
I miss her—who I was before it all ended.

*"Brothers, I do not consider myself yet to have
taken hold of it. But one thing I do forgetting what is
behind and straining toward what is ahead I press on
toward the goal to win the prize for which God has
called me" – Phil 3:13-14, New International Version.*

*Leesa Ward has always had a call on her life. At a
very young age, she felt as though she was to accomplish something bigger than the vision she had been
given by her family and friends.*

*"In my early years, I went through some very
difficult times, but I believe now that God uses those
things for us to grow so that we can become stronger
accomplish more and help others. It is going through
the deepest Valley that I have grown and through those
challenges which my character has been shaped. One
of my favorite sayings is 'prayer is answered not by
being given what we asked for but challenged to be all
that we can be'. I think too many people stop short of
living life fully, not utilizing all their gifts and talents."*

*In 1988, at the age of twenty-three, Leesa started her real estate career at Century 21 in Tracy. Being the top producer her first year out of fourteen agents, she was approached by her mentor, Vina Albright, to join her in opening Albright Realty. Leesa and Vina worked together for over five years, and this was instrumental in Leesa's life as she nurtured her own dream of expanding her business and taking it to the next level.*

*"I am thankful that I didn't know what I didn't know when I first started out. I have always been an all or nothing person, which helped drive me even when faced with fear."*

*The things that stop most people, however, are the things that motivate Leesa. She left Albright Realty and worked out of RE/MAX for six years, continuing her success by occupying three office suites to accommodate her clients and support team of one buyer's agent and an escrow coordinator. Still, she longed to take full control and build a company that was based on the Christian principles that are the foundation of her life, thus providing a working environment that is meaningful and joyous allowing everyone to share in the wealth and success. Most importantly, she wanted everyone to feel loved, accepted, and encouraged to be all that they could be in their business and personal lives.*

*"Life is too short and too long to dread going to work and hate what you're doing, especially when we*

spend the majority of our waking hours doing it. I love waking up to each new day. It is truly a gift."

Leesa left RE/MAX and in a step of faith bought an old Wells Fargo bank building that had sat vacant downtown for over five years.

"I was so excited buying this building even though I had been advised against it by both friends and colleagues. I just felt that downtown would always be the heart and core of Tracy and with all of the improvement and renovation taking place I could not go wrong. I'm glad I took the risk."

Today when you walk through the doors into the splendidly remodeled building of Ward Real Estate at 1034 Central Avenue, Tracy, all of your senses are pleasantly engaged as you listen to running waterfalls, view tropical palms, and other colorful plants amid the sound of real Amazon parrots. The walls speak confidently of Leesa's faith in God, and her love for encouraging quotations. The largest of these is a six foot by four foot by Henry Thoreau that states "Go confidently in the direction of your dreams. Live the life you've imagined."

"I think it's an excellent reminder not only for my agents but for everyone who sets foot in our office."

Leesa's office is also a statement of her belief in God that has never failed to guide and direct her, even when she admitted she couldn't understand why the *path at times with so steep and rocky. She is bold in sharing that faith, quick to point out that it has been her strength, giving credit to the Lord for an office that now employs eleven buyers' agents, two escrow coordinators, as well as a staff totaling twenty-one in all, dedicated customer service personnel. Leesa admits that it still overwhelms her when she drives into the parking lot of her building and is humbled to see Ward Real Estate at the top of it.*

*"I really do believe all things are possible regardless of the circumstances in what might appear to be faithfully true. I do not want to take credit for what others might think I have achieved alone. I would be nothing without my faithful and loyal team. No one at Ward Real Estate is more important than the other. I own the company together with my partner and best friend Alison Jensen and I am blessed to be able to work with my sister Athena. Everyone here is valuable.*

*We all work together as a team and family, and it is truly a blessing and reward to experience the miracles of people growing and maturing right before one's eyes. We have a blast here every day." Leesa Ward is a successful energetic businesswoman and enthusiastic mom who loves her three children, Taylor, Thomas, and Baelee, and is an active supporter of the crisis pregnancy center in Tracy. She loves music – a must at her meetings. Leesa also loves to write, especially her ongoing journals for each of her children, a gift to them when they are older. She is also working on her first book, and it appears one of her personal goals is to meet Oprah.*

*"I just love her and think she is an incredible woman who has accomplished so much. She has strength and status and yet has an extremely humble spirit who loves to give. Looking back, there were many people who influenced and helped me acquire the tools and foundations for achieving in this business. Sometimes it was just encouraging words or the way someone went out of their way to share their experience with me, like Vina, proving that the way she did business, one can be financially successful and prosper without sacrificing values. Wanda Sullivan showed me that everyone wants, needs and deserves to feel like the most important person in the world."*

*Leesa utilizes an established master plan in her marketing strategy and a systematic approach that addresses all phases of the real estate business as a whole. This offers and encourages each client the opportunity to make informed decisions whether they are buying, selling or investing. It simply answers all the questions and makes Ward Real Estate a complete resource center. Her mentoring program includes weekly accountability and brainstorming workshops that involve her entire office. Although she wants her* company to grow, Leesa says that it will not be at the expense of the team or the overall marketing concept that she has worked so hard to implement.

"It's very important that the agents we hire, regardless of experience, share mutual goals, values, and are equally driven by passion for this business and the people they serve, not their ego."

Leesa's desire is to make a difference and help others seek their highest potential whether it's encouraging employee, help for a seller in a distressing situation, or putting someone who never thought they could buy a home into one. She also actively invests by purchasing property either in a foreclosure situation or a home that needs renovation, which she says not only helps improve the neighborhood and community, but she also provides a nice home with creative financing options for many home buyers. Her own words, however, best sum up her life both personally and professionally.

"The most important thing to me is being real. I have come to that juncture in my life where have accepted myself not because of my name, my business status or my success but because I am a child of God, created for a reason and a purpose. I do my best each day to live accordingly. Doing and standing up for what is right is so important, even if you are the only one standing."

*Leesa continues with assurance, knowing that this is her life's work and true calling and though the vehicle is her real estate company, it's really about so much more.*

*Based on the many letters that Leesa and her colleagues at Ward Real Estate received from thankful clients and the comments directly from her staff and agents, I am confident that doing what is right openly and honestly is still the best principle upon which to build a successful business.*

I always knew I wanted to be and do something big. I was born that way. I always had this sense of urgency, maybe because I always thought I was going to die young for some reason. I wanted to make a big change, to stand out from the norm, not for some fame or uplifted ego, but to really make a bold statement and a movement that would change the way people operate in their business and treat each other – love and respect versus ugly competitor mentality. This is especially hard in the real estate business since everybody works on commission, and every day you're basically unemployed until you obtain a new client, buyer, or seller. It was cutthroat with empty promises in order to get the listing from the seller, only for them to find out that they really did need to paint the house and install new carpet like I told them.

And the price range is what it is. Based on market facts, property sold like kind, adjustments made based on amenities and improvements within, and where it's located. This is how it will be appraised. You can't sell AT&T stocks for fifteen dollars a share when they're only going for ten. Some sellers put their faith in what they want to believe and the agent gives that to them. Obviously, with being a small city outside the Silicon Valley Bay area, where people would flock and surely drive the commute in order to buy a home that was sometimes more than half the cost and with more to offer. It was a dog-eat-dog mentality with both the agents and clients. There was competition even when the Bay Area market slowed. We had a market that was in demand and always in shortage. I always operated with truth and honesty regardless of whether or not I got the listing or worked with a buyer because it's the right thing. Buyers and sellers depend on you, their families depend on you, as well as their goals and dreams and all the necessary obligations they have, like work, school or important events.

They need to feel secure, certain that they can make plans based on the expectations that you told them they could depend on. I would always meet with the client and just be absolutely real with them, telling them things they don't necessarily want to hear but being honest about their situation, their house, the market, and the reality based on comps and recorded closings of what their house would most likely sell for. It wasn't just my opinion – I had documented facts to show and prove what I was saying and explaining, examples of other transactions, good and bad, so that ultimately, they could make an educated decision and not just one out of emotion or taking the advice of a less than transparent agent. That doesn't serve anybody.

You can be strong without force but instead, out of the love you have for the people you serve. Then when your intention is in the right place, coming from truth and heart, everything aligns and magic happens.

## The Behind the Scenes

During the years that led up to me finally putting up my son Taylor into a residential treatment facility for Reactive Attachment Disorder (RAD), I was pretty much on my own. I had his father and his then-wife working against me, and the counselors and doctors all had their different opinions and diagnosis - quick with wanting to treat symptoms. He was on several different medications since they thought at first he had OCD or Tourette's Syndrome, along with many other possibilities. At that time, I was completely against any kind of medication or drugs, especially for a young boy.

During one of his visitations at his father's home, my ex-husband's wife took him to the doctors where she signed and authorized him to be put on Risperdall and Depakote, based on what she told the doctor the issues were. It wasn't until he was back at my home that I was informed he was now taking these medications and the times I needed to administer them. I was so pissed and could not believe that she was able to do that without my authorization or consent. I met with the doctor after I read up on everything I could, front and back, making sure I understood every single definition, ingredient, side effect, or any possible ramification because I was determined to ultimately wean him off the drugs. I met with Doctor Wong, and she was completely taken back as she showed me the signature on the consent form signed by the new wife as Taylor's mother. Within one month, Taylor was completely lethargic, falling asleep sitting up, and ballooned with an additional twenty-five pounds on his little nine-year-old body. Why was I the only one who thought there was something seriously wrong with this picture?

I felt it was just a way for everybody to take the easy way out - teachers, parents, authorities - with having him on medication verses trying to enforce behavioral standards. However, after all of the intense self-education I invested in and a weekend workshop with Nancy Thomas, who worked with thousands of kids giving them a chance to heal and learn to love and trust, as well as giving the parents hope that things could be different and their child could grow up to be decent and responsible adults, I knew what I had to do if I wanted to be able to give Taylor a chance. I searched out several different facilities supposedly specializing in RAD kids and troubled boys. My insurance would cover the expense only if it was located in California. Unfortunately, most were located outside the state and the one that truly represented what was needed to treat his disorder, was located in Quincy, Illinois. It was extremely expensive, almost $20,000 a month, which included his room and board, school, medication, and the expense of me visiting to do counseling and therapy with him every four to six weeks. There is absolutely nothing that can prepare you for that - taking your child to another state, leaving him with strangers, and knowing that it will be a constant strict, new environment that he would have no choice but to live in for the next eighteen months to two years, depending on his progress. It was an emotional roller coaster, even for me - when I thought I was pretty strong.

## Shaky Beginnings

In addition to coping with Taylor and all the wonderful surprises that came along with it, I had just opened up my own real estate company, with someone I had a previous business relationship with for over five years. Kimberly was my preferred lender I used to help my buyers obtain financing to buy their homes. She also helped me fund all of my homes and investment properties. It was pretty easy back then - if you had good credit and could fog a mirror, you got a loan. She had her own mortgage company in Stockton and lived in Lodi, so when she approached wanting to work with me in Tracy, it didn't make sense.

I asked her, "Why would you be willing to commute back-and-forth and give up all your other real-estate agent clients because of the fact that we would be working together as one team?"

She responded, "Because, Leesa, you are my number one client. Eighty-five percent of my business comes from you alone. I know we can do something so big together."

"Wow," I thought. "She saw something in me. She's got to know what she's talking about, right?"

She's smart, valedictorian of her Humphrey Law school class. I was really excited! Scared, like you are when anything is new, but excited. I began renovating and transforming a Wells Fargo bank building into an office in commitment to this new and thrilling endeavor, with Kimberly now joining me. It wasn't long before our partnership dissolved-within ten months, which resulted in a long year of negotiating and pretty much giving her whatever she wanted, despite all the property we as a company owned, that was being purchased with *my* money, made through *my* negotiations, connections, resources, and *my* credit, etc. Nothing really mattered to me except for my name, company logo, phone number, and at least half the properties that I bought. It was ok. I knew I could do it all over again. I was established, knew the business, the market, had great relationships and network. I knew I'd be able to survive and thrive regardless if I had anything. Kimberly, on the other hand, had nothing to lose. I seriously felt sorry for her. I just wanted it done and over with so we could just move on once and for all.

I really wanted to be able to get back to work, settle my office and all of the employees down, make them feel safe and comfortable, and get things back into order. I felt so bad for everybody. It was stressful, chaotic, and every day, there was something new as far as drama. The employees were confused and divided, not knowing who to listen to, myself or Kimberly. It disrupted how we interacted with each other, our trust, as well as the ability to focus and be productive and engage with our clients.

Every day, I'd worry about something happening that would disrupt our business and the people we served. I was also concerned about the reputation of the company. Some days, it was slamming and locking doors; other days there was calling the police, and others with U-Haul trucks showing up with her and movers stripping out half of the furniture, décor, business and office supplies, etc. My adrenaline was working on over drive - on edge nonstop. I couldn't sleep, couldn't eat, and I was down to ninety-seven pounds—with muscle, by the way.

This is where you have to really, truly listen to your intuition- your gut, God speaking, that tingly feeling of knowing something is off or something is wrong; and yet the majority of us choose to ignore and push those feelings aside out of guilt for even having them in the first place. I honestly felt that there was something just not quite right.

I knew - I totally knew but didn't want to believe what I was feeling. I tried justifying and reverted back to using logical common sense to counteract my non-scientifically, calculated feelings. Why is it that we go against ourselves, and we don't trust what we don't think is factual or measurable by society's standards? My inner knowing has proven me right time and time again, but still, I hesitate, trusting in more than just myself.

## Finally Smooth Sailing

After my experience with Kimberly and all the repercussions that came with the admission to part ways, I had the freedom to continue the pursuit of my business but on my own terms. I had thirty-three investors who believed in me, my company, and the ability to continue the success for everyone involved. Most were people who knew me or my partner Alison, saw what we were doing, and wanted to be a part of it. I offered twelve percent, with a straight note, typically for a ten-year contract. This enabled me to buy homes in distress situations, directly from sellers, pre-fore-closure and at the Trustee courthouse auction, which only allowed all-cash bids and purchases. There was a lot of money involved, over eleven million dollars. I had a financial advisor and attorneys that oversaw the agreements and assured me that everything was in order and law-abiding. If there was any other license or certification I needed, I would have easily gotten it. I had perfect credit, a thriving company, and a rep-utation I would have never risked. My business and clients were my life.

## The Beginning of the End

When my sister took control of the company, there were lots of changes that took place I wasn't even aware of. Her husband also worked for the company, overseeing the construction part of the homes being renovated. There were employees that were termi-nated, agents who left, and investors that were panick-ing with not being able to speak with me directly. My cell phone and computer were taken, and employees were forbidden from trying to contact me, allowing me the ability to completely let go and concentrate on taking care of my son.

After my personal assistant was let go, she became very bitter; she wanted the company to pay her a $60,000 "exit fee". When that didn't happen, out of spite, she contacted all my investors and told them the business was going down and they should get their money out while they could. You can imagine what happened after that.

Everybody panicked and wanted their investment returned. Even though we had a contract for a specific amount of time, obviously, it's not like the bank account was holding the money. It was utilized to buy real estate and was tied up as equity or in the renovation process. We averaged twenty-five to thirty homes a month. I wouldn't have been able to pay twelve-percent interest if I wasn't utilizing it and didn't make money. It just didn't make sense. Keeping money in the bank didn't make sense.

I wasn't aware of the severity of what was going on until the beginning of 2007. Bills weren't getting paid, and my water was turned off. I received a phone call asking when I would be able to make a payment since my car payment was two or three months behind. What?? I didn't feel right driving a car I wasn't paying for, so I drove it to the dealership and gave them the keys instead of them having to do a formal repossession. I was devastated knowing my credit was going to be affected, to say the least. In addition to finding out little-by-little of what was taking place at the office, I learned that there were eight lawsuits from investors. Our real estate attorney was trying to mitigate and keep things manageable, but our demise was inevitable sooner or later.

"Oh my Gosh, Athena," I thought, "What the heck is going on? I want to speak to the attorney myself. I need to know details if I'm trying to jump in and work through what is going on and needs to be addressed."

It's amazing how everyone wants to cover their own butts when it all goes down, including our attorney, who was so-called "representing" us. I wanted her to catch me up to speed with what was transpiring, that I was stepping back in and that she was to deal with me now versus my sister. When she refused, not wanting to reiterate the past few months, I asked her, "Do I need to find another attorney?"

She replied, "I know more about your business than you do right now." Now, I was also panicking. No, I take that back, I was freaking the freak out!

I didn't know exactly what was happening. I wanted and needed to know if I was going to be able to try and pull things together. I was instructed not to contact and try to resolve things with my investors directly myself since they had representation. I can only imagine how they felt and what they were going through since they had trusted me with such large amounts of money, savings or withdrawals from CDs, and some even took out lines of credit on their homes.

Again, I was totally freaking out. My partner and I had always paid our investors first and foremost and always on time. Our relationship and trust were extremely important to us. The majority of the investments were from our own family members as well, especially my partner Alison's family. And just for the record, none of our own family members or the larger business investors that we had worked with for many years filed a lawsuit or went to the DA to try and prosecute.

Needless to say, things continued to escalate out of control. I had multiple lawsuits from investors, having to go through bankruptcy and was eventually incarcerated and standing trial with forty-eight counts of felony charges. Totally unreal.

To this day, I have not spoken with Athena since March of 2007—twelve years. It's not that I dislike or hate her. I truly feel that she did all she was able and capable of doing. I know she tried-until it got to be too much. I guess the thing that hurts me the most is, I didn't feel she stuck up for me or stood by my side when I was going through the hardest time of my life, when I needed her most. When it got hard and too much, I feel she had abandoned me. I don't want to accuse or blame, point the finger, or push off any responsibility that I should have taken, being the owner of the company, but in addition to everything I was going through, I felt really alone. I lost a sister—her choice, over the events that took place.

After a strong dose of Prozac and not wanting to risk twelve jurors not being able to comprehend the amount of money going in and out of my business, in addition to possibly having a bad experience dealing with a real estate broker or home transaction, I accepted a plea bargain with the DA for a three year house arrest sentence.

So many changes and a life I never thought could happen to me was now my reality. It's been thirteen years… thirteen long-fricken years of agony, guilt, worthlessness, devastation, self-punishment, shame and just wanting to be invisible. It isn't me. I know I wasn't meant to play small, but how do I even begin to move on and feel good when I know I've caused such catastrophic occurrences and have hurt so many people? Where do I even start? The thing that allowed me to give to others is now the thing that has taken so much away. How can I ever *really* feel good again?

I have spent tens of thousands of dollars (well actually, my boyfriend did) trying to get the right answers in order for me to move forward with no avail, anything from self-employed entrepreneurs, psychologists, coaches, master-mind marketing groups and other professionals, with the intent of discovering how to start over *and* feel good. I knew there was no other option. There was no way that I could do *anything* without first and foremost releasing myself of the guilt and shame of my past, and feeling worthy enough to engage with people again. I needed to see past my past, my life that was currently in shambles and torn to shreds.

## Being Arrested

The whole city and outskirts of San Joaquin County Valley, had memories and was etched in my heart and soul. How could it not be in the forefront of my mind as well? The city, businesses, neighborhoods and people I've spent twenty plus years developing relationships with. It was my work, my life; the city was my office.

I couldn't be or go anywhere that didn't remind me, that didn't make me feel like an outcast, alone, left behind with everyone else carrying on with their lives. I was left to observe, think, and ponder the aftermath and everyone else's current reality I was no longer a part of.

While planning a move to Southern California in hopes to move on from this devastation for a fresh start, I was selling what little I had left on craigslist and a yard sale I posted and was getting ready for, my eighty-one-year-old mother was clearly showing a steady rate of Alzheimer's.

It seemed to come on and continue to escalate faster and faster every day. I was now trying to care for a 150-pound infant that I couldn't easily carry around with me in a baby seat or stroller. She also liked to make a scene for attention anytime, anywhere. Regardless, it was never enough. She was in her own world and wanted everyone to join her to accommodate it. That was the day I finally took my mom to senior day care so I could get some packing done without worrying about her falling. It was also the day I got arrested.

I was outside with a cigarette in one hand and a spray can in another. I had already advertised what I was selling and made sure it was all going getting priced at that point to guarantee there would be nothing left over at the end of the day. I noticed a car parked about approximately 200 feet away. I kept doing my thing, assuming it was somebody who wanted to scope out the stuff I was setting up for the morning sale. After a while, it started to bug me. I was feeling like there was something, off and my guard was up at this point since I'd had to watch my back now for over two plus years.

Finally, I walked over to the car and boldly asked, "Can I help you with something? You've been sitting here for over an hour now."

And she said, "Yeah, actually, I have come regarding the senior abuse."

"Wait, what? Can I see your card?"

She said, "Yes, as soon as you put your cigarette and spray paint can down."

"Really??" I dropped them both. She got out of the car and the next thing I know, she grabbed me and threw me against the hood, huffing and puffing, and bound me with handcuffs. "What? Stop it! What the flip is going on??"

Obviously, she lied and placed me under arrest. I never had been arrested or in any kind of trouble before besides getting a speeding ticket, and here I was, in the back of an undercover car, handcuffed a little too tight I might add...waiting for back up to help transfer me due to me being so "hostile."

While I was trying to get answers from the DA, she was calling for backup to get assistance with handling and transferring me to be booked. *Hostile? Wow, seriously? Me, five feet tall, 110 pounds? Yeah, such a threat.* Something happens though when your adrenaline is jacked up to its limit and on overdrive. You become fearless and bold. Like, what's the worst thing that could happen? I was already in handcuffs waiting to find out what the inside of a jail house looks like.

Absolutely unreal. I didn't have time for this, number one, and was wondering how long this whole arrest thing and going down this station was going to take, since I had all my stuff outside and still had to prepare for the sale in the morning. Most pressing and stressful, I needed to pick up my mom at day care by 5:00 p.m. I asked her again how long this was going to take, calculating the half hour drive to in from Stockton and then whatever it takes to be booked. I need to be able to pick up my mom. She said, "So then let's hurry it along."

## At the Station

I've always had a problem with trust. In fact, even the people I wasn't that close to and my agents would state, "You have an issue." Yeah, I do. Everybody in my life has let me down. I can only depend on myself. I was the only sure thing that I was able to control. So I thought. That kind of talk makes God laugh out loud.

I have learned there are so very few things that you can count on, that are solid and can depend your life upon. One of those things is my Uncle Jimmy. He is eighty-eight years old and emotionally, financially, and physically supports so many people in his life – family, friends, and anybody else he thinks needs a helping hand. Thank God he's had the same phone number for sixty-five years because when you're incarcerated, they don't allow you to use your phone, and who knows anyone's number by heart anymore since it's all programmed? But luckily, when they said you get a phone call, I was able to remember my Aunt Gloria and Uncle Jimmy's phone number to call for help and let them know where I was and what was going on. The system, at that time anyway, didn't allow you to call or leave a voice message on a cell phone number. Who has a home landline phone number anymore? My Aunt Gloria and Uncle Jimmy.

I won't even get into the whole booking, shuffling through the stalls and barricades of the shifting system and what it was like being booked inside a place I never thought I would see. That's a complete other book alone. But I will tell you that there is nothing like the experience of been roughhoused with nothing you could do it about it. You have no voice, no rights. You are a nothing person who happens to be going through the workday of Ms. Tough as Nails, who clearly wants to let you know who was boss from the start. You're basically just like a zombie being pushed through the lines, getting shots, taking blood, asking you questions like do you have any tattoos, stripping you down, turning over all your possessions, and then wearing somebody else's ten-times too big underwear, socks, orange jumpsuit, and rubber flip flops.

I kept telling them that I'm not going be staying, and there was a mistake. I need to pick up my mom, and this was only supposed to take an hour; but they weren't listening. They kept yelling at me: "Ward, get over here! Ward, sit down! Ward, stand up! Ward, move it along!"

*Oh my gosh, are you kidding me? Do they know who I am? I'm not the drug pusher or the murderer here. I'm a decent businesswoman who has been wrongly accused of...* well... things you can obviously be incarcerated for.

It was so surreal, to say the least. I remember walking down a hall, not even believing what was taking place. I felt like I was in a dream—or a nightmare. It was so ridiculous I wanted to start laughing and crying out loud. People can do that when they're uncomfortable you know.

I was then placed in a five-by-eight-foot cell with a small camping-type cot, a stainless-steel sink, and a toilet with no lid. I had a roommate who was about nineteen years old, who was obviously on drugs and kept throwing up in the toilet that happened to be next to the head of my sleeping floor area.

It didn't take long for me to get in trouble shortly after when I was simply looking out the three-by-twenty-four-inch window just to see what time it was, like it even mattered. The guard said I was smirking at her, so I was in confinement for twenty-four hours.

That was day one. I was there for thirteen long, torturous, wouldn't-wish-it-on-my-own-worst-enemy days. And don't even get me started on the disgusting baloney that you eat day after day.

Again, that's a whole other book.

## House Arrest

Obviously, there is so much in between, but to sum everything that took place with my company, it resulted in years of cases and trials. The first one was actually dismissed, and then the DA filed again, which they're able to do if the first judge dismisses for some reason. I don't know, but I do know he was able to do it.

In the meantime, I've had a five-pound lock box/ GPS on my ankle from the time I was arrested, on bail, going through trial, and for the next three years of my sentence of house arrest, after myself and my partner agreed to settle with the DA. Neither one of us could handle another day in court or depending on a jury to determine our fate. There was so much involved and even though it killed us, crying our eyes out as we were initialing and signing the statements of what we were "guilty" of, we knew there was no other choice if we were even thinking about trying to move on.

In between all of this were bankruptcy court dates with victims able to show up and yell profanity at you while you sit there, trying to pretend it doesn't hurt. And then going to all the lawsuits hearings that were filed against me, seeing my clients/the victims in court – it was so devastating. I remember Pastor Brown and his wife came up to me in the lobby and said, "Leesa, we trusted you."

I said, "I know, I know. I'm so sorry."

And then they replied, "And we still do."

We embraced as I sobbed uncontrollably. I literally went home and wrote in my journal, thanking God for the miracle of that encounter.

It was so hard being in such a formal setting with such legal consequences with the people I loved, the people I only wanted the best for, the people I knew that depended on me, the people that had faith and trust in me for their future, their livelihood. I would have to say, out of everything, that was probably the hardest for me.

There is absolutely no way I don't cringe or feel like an ice pick is being plunged through my heart when I hear anything involving money, houses, moving, investment, banks, mortgages, interest rate, retirement, buying, selling, business, start up, fixer upper, reno-vations, construction, office building, commercial, tax deduction, guarantee, contract, 401K , CRT attorney, bankruptcy, foreclosure, for sale, open houses, subdivision, neighborhoods, escrow, title, closing, cash to close, down payment, gift, co-signer, joint tenants, disclosures, FSBO, run down, abandon houses, tall grass, weeds, MLS, watching HGTV, commercials… OK, so pretty much everything I see, hear, and participate in, there is no escaping what I used to do. It took me a year and a half to even drive by my building after everything crumbled.

## Ward Building

My once so beautiful office, once with so much life, was now being abandoned as well. Things were being stolen out of it, and the grounds, trees and flowers were displaying the lack of care and attention it once knew. Somebody even bombed it—thank God I was not there –they had placed it right outside my window.

It made me so sad thinking about how much hate was swirling around with my name and face associated with it. All the good I worked so hard for, the love I gave so freely to everyone I met and worked with, was now worth nothing. Not even remembered. I was not even given the benefit of the doubt. I was guilty of all of the horrible things that were stated as facts.

It wasn't just me who suffered but also all of my employees, some of whom were the sole providers for their families. A few of them continued to work there even though they were not getting paid just out of loyalty. In addition, they also had to deal with angry clients or investors who walked in wanting to get answers and speak with me.

My partner and I lost our homes to foreclosure as well as all of the investment properties. How ironic, when that was my business... real estate, helping and assisting distressed sellers and their homes in foreclosure and here I am with all of my properties in default and foreclosured upon but that's what happens when you're depressed. You can't think. You don't even know what to do. I mean, here I am, Miss Specialist when it comes to all of this, and I was frozen and paralyzed and had no one to turn to. I felt as if the whole community and even my peers were just sitting back, watching it unravel, watching everything unravel, and nobody felt comfortable I guess, to step up and reach out. Not that it's their obligation or that I deserved anything other than what was going on; I'm just saying it's sad.

Who I was and everything I'd ever done and maintained for over two decades didn't matter. It was as though people wanted to believe what the media made me out to be or were glad I had fallen so hard.

It never let up. It all continued to escalate every day. People coming to my house—people I didn't even know. I was concerned about my kids. I felt completely exposed, unsafe, knowing that everyone knew who I was even if I didn't know them.

# Chapter 3:

# Stepping Stones

When you are consumed and take on the new identity of "failure" or a loser, it affects you personally, as well as your family and loved ones. Trying to pick yourself back up and feel validated when you feel low and worthless is hard... when your self-esteem has been destroyed, crushed, and washed away by a single incident or failure. Your spouse, significant other and close friends all look at you and treat you differently, which only reinforces how you feel and the way you act in turn. It's a never ending cycle until you finally do realize, that you aren't the person they fell in love with....you are no longer who they admired and had so much in common with. No longer bouncing around with endless enthusiasm or speaking with the proficient vocabulary you once did. Can you really blame them? You don't even recognize yourself. It's all so painful and again, so lonely.

## Lonely at the Top

When they say it's lonely at the top, it is. I don't know if you truly understand that until you're at the top looking down and feel like there isn't anybody you can look up to. This is also definitely a problem when you have so many people depending on you—when you're the leader, owner, and instructor. You're supposed to be strong and have all the answers.

I remember the day my sister Athena walked out to the back of my office where I was trying to hide and cry without anybody noticing. Athena had worked with me and my real estate company for eight years. I don't even think she's ever seen me cry.

When she came out and saw me crying, she freaked out. "Oh my gosh, what's the matter with you? You're my rock."

How sad and scary this must be for anybody who depends on somebody else to be their strength, their warrior, someone that's going to handle everything so all you need to do is move along and do what you're supposed to and everything works out.

Afterwards, she told me, "Leesa, you've taken care of everybody for so many years. Now, let me take care of you."

I don't know if that's the exact day that she realized that I was falling apart or if it was just confirmation of what she already knew, but it was the beginning of me acknowledging that I couldn't handle things at that point.

## Disturbing Signs

There were some very disturbing signs with Taylor, which questioned my beliefs on what was "normal" I've always been a journalist, so I've written and doc-umented daily events, prayers, etc. for as long as I can remember. Taylor was my first child, so I didn't know what was typical or if that was the way it is with kids, but it made me never want to have another child. It was seven years later that I gave birth to Thomas and seventeen months after his birth that I had my sweet angel, Baelee.

I am so thankful I didn't keep thinking that having children meant your life was full of stress and heartache and that was just the way it was being a mother. I feel guilty even talking about this, and even though I've always wanted to write a book, I knew I would wait until my mother passed away because I didn't want to hurt her feelings. Now I'm worried about hurting my son's feelings, but good news, he doesn't read.

This is where documenting is so important. Misconceptions and perspectives are so different for everybody. The same circumstances yield different results and different meanings for everybody involved.

I keep thinking if my mother journaled, if I was able to read her feelings and thoughts and everything that she was going through, I would totally understand and appreciate them, and it would have helped me get over some of things from my childhood. It's why I have separate journal books for each child. So regardless of what they think happened or how they want interpret what they think happened, I've got my thoughts feelings written down so at least they can know my true heart, versus what may be on their mind or what a counselor would tell them when they're sitting there, thirty plus years old and wanting to blame their mother for their miserable life.

It's been an ongoing joke with Baelee and Thomas about how people change. I kept writing letters and little notes – "I know you love me now, but it's going to change." I always wanted them to have the best childhood memories. I was consumed with making sure that they could look back and feel loved and secure and have good thoughts when thinking back on their childhood and their mom. Like most people my age, I imagine we all have some horror story and experiences we can share about how hard we had it growing up, how abusive mom or dad was, how unloved we felt, if we only had things different or brought up in another family.

My point is we all have issues, problems, circumstances of events that have shaped our lives. We can sit, dwell, blame, and make excuses for why we are the way we are, while giving ourselves permission to really not do anything; or we can decide we are in control of our lives. It's up to us, and there's no one else to blame. Yes, it's true, things would have been different if I was born into another family, and sometimes I get mad or jealous. Then I think, "Wow, you don't even appreciate what you have." But, like Wayne Dyer says, we are all born into the family that we chose to be born into. So when you're a Christian and you read The Bible and follow those principles, it's very difficult to wrap your mind around, "Why would I want to be in this situation?" But he goes on to say that we chose because we want to evolve and become everything we were meant to be and to overcome obstacles and learn the life lessons that are important.

P.S.—My very favorite author as well is Deepak Chopra. He is very deep, and it takes a minute to even be able to comprehend and digest, but he's brilliant. He's a doctor/scientist, like Dr Dyer and wanted to leave his practice because he felt called to do something more important... helping and teaching others to awaken spiritually.

He has totally confirmed my feelings and beliefs with, just because it was in my heart, that I understood our intuition is more real than our so-called logical thought. Our minds try to wrap things around what we can make sense of—period - but a lot of times, it works against you. We need to trust more in our intuition, guidance, God, and spirit-filled energy, versus what people state is scientific facts. I truly believe that the world and people are now evolving more into the smart, spiritual, intuitive, and awakened beings that we were meant to be. When I read old books from the 1800s or 1900s I think, "Oh my goodness, they were so smart back then. We're still learning stuff based on what they've achieved and learned intuitively and yet, we think we're so smart because of how we have undeniably evolved and grown, with all the technology that exists."

## Forgiveness of Self and Others

So how do you overcome this humiliation, shame, loss of identity, and depression? You start by forgiving yourself and those you feel betrayed you. In this book, you'll learn how to start over and walk with your head up high, move on, and stop living in the past - beating yourself up, wishing it was different, and running the same movie and song over and over in your head. You're trying to handle losing your reputation, community, self-worth, social circles, losing your friends or at least who you thought were friends.

Dr. Wayne Dyer talks about how we seek respect, as well as, care about our reputation and what others think of us, more than we should. In order for us to be self-actualized individuals, it is necessary to be "independent of the good opinions of others," but it's hard when you're human and want acceptance and approval. It's always been a struggle for me and is difficult to do when your business depends on your character and morals, a.k.a. your reputation, to grow and thrive. You want everyone to know that you're a good person, you're ethical, and they can trust you. It's hard.

## Responsibility and Accountability

Facing up to what happened is not going to change anything. It's you that has to. Yes, I know. It seems impossible to feel anything other than the pain, suffering, and humiliation you feel right now. It's the hardest and worst thing you've ever gone through, and you've gone through a lot. So how do you get over it? What do you do, and where do you even begin when the only life you knew and loved is gone?

Let's get real and do something different. Obviously, nothing has changed and doing nothing is just not working. There comes a day, hopefully sooner than later, where you realize there's no more hiding. You have no more excuses. There are no more timeouts or days left to dwell and reminisce about what once was, what went wrong, or what you could have done differently. We can't keep living in the past and using our misfortunes as a way to live small and get out of the responsibility.

Trust me, it's a waste of time if all you're contributing to the world is just breathing the air. It doesn't last and only delays the inevitable. You have to do something different. The sooner you get back out there, the sooner you can move on with living instead of just existing.

Sometimes life is just one big, wild, crazy mess, one day to the next day, and you're just waiting for the moment you can stop, breathe, and take inventory. You keep thinking that once you get a "break," you can stop, analyze, reboot, then start to motivate and make new plans to just start all over again. But the next thing you know, it's been years and you're still in the same place. There is no break or timeout in life, and if you fall into this trap, you'll realize you've done nothing and are far from moving on.

It's a hard pill to swallow when you realize how much time you've lost - time from your life, a commodity you can never recover between where you were and where you still are. It's a big "come-to-Jesus" moment, and you may find yourself wondering *What? Seriously? How did I end up here? Me? I can't believe I am still stuck in the same place, thinking the same things - lost.* But the good news is that it's the perfect foundation for building your new life, the starting point to assess where you are.

Throughout this book, I will show you how you've allowed your past to keep you stuck and unable to move forward, keeping you in the loop cycle of where you are and how to finally break the chains that bind you. "Busy" work doesn't mean you've pushed the reset button and are starting over, beginning a new zest for life. Most of the time we just don't know *what* to do. I will be including examples throughout, disclosing all of the hidden gems we use to distract ourselves day after day, and sometimes, believing our own lies we tell ourselves.

Buddha once said, "We are what we think. All that we are arises with our thoughts, which in turn, determines our actions, which ultimately results in our destination."

Obviously, we all need to take responsibility for where we are and the choices and decisions that we've made over the years. Every thought has an action, which creates a reaction or result. It's a total compound effect, like how the doubling of a penny, compounded every day, will actually leave you with five million dollars after thirty days. Unbelievable, but that's also exactly what happens with our days/lives as well. And sometimes the action/reaction turn out completely different than what you would have ever imagined, planned for, or expected. However, we can't keep using that as an excuse to give up. We need to continue to be consistent- everyday, regardless of what we may or may not see immediately. We'll get into that in the following chapters.

You start questioning and wondering, *Who am I and now what?*

Yeah, now what? There was no plan B; this was it. This was your life. And now, for whatever circumstances you're going through, you're left with shame and humiliation, unable to even begin to think about how you'll get out of this mess; or how to even start to move forward without the basic foundation of confidence and self-esteem. Insecurities and doubt are at the forefront, leaving you paralyzed and preventing you from making any decisions to start over fresh, let alone even with something as simple as - like what to have for dinner.

## What's Great about This? Ask the Right Questions

Asking the right questions and using positive words when structuring them, versus negativity, makes all the difference in how you feel, the energy you have when implementing your new goals, and the actual vibrations you create. This literally propels the Universe to conspire on your behalf with you being able to achieve your focused desire. It only takes seventeen seconds of conscious, good thoughts to change your emotions, thus allowing you draw to you whatever you focus on. But, you have to choose to change your thoughts- on purpose, even when you feel bad and would rather just wallow in self pity...or not think at all.

If you're anything like me, you've gotten to the point of trying not to hurt or wanting to numb yourself just to get through the day of doing nothing. You feel so completely different than who you used to be. (I've used that very word more than anyone should, another word I hate − yes hate. "Trying" is another one. Either do it or don't. Trying to pick up that rock is not really doing it. Try − it's not a yes or a no, didn't or did; it's only "trying.")

Numbing myself daily with alcohol was one vice, and an addiction I thought would never be a part of my life story but it became another life changing obstacle I'd have to battle.

No, I was the control freak − coffee, Red Bull, cigarettes (fyi, I no longer smoke)- but not alcohol. Eating disorder, but not alcohol. Workaholic, but not an alcoholic. The once or twice a year glass of wine thing I did have or when I drank on special occasions, made me feel less than on top of my game. Less than sharp-minded, less than assertively in control. But when you've lost everything, including your self-worth and identity, there is nothing left to control, no life purpose or passion. Nothing.

I loved the alcohol numbing, the effortless blank thought of nothing, physically and mentally. But like any addiction, it took more and more to reach that state of being content with just existing, to block all the feelings and emotions. It took drinking more often—daily, hourly - until it was the very first thing I did in the morning. Gin, bourbon, and vodka gladly took the place of my coffee ritual. Of course, I was going to stop. I just needed a little help to get over this hump I couldn't seem to jump over and move through; but just as easy as it was to be emotionally addicted, my physical body followed suit.

It was hard to function without it. Thoughts of drinking consumed my mind always, thinking about how to sneak and conceal it, or if I had enough to last me the day. I kept track of the stores I had last gone to and planned my shopping accordingly, hoping it wasn't written all over my face and that I could stop shaking long enough to punch in my debit card code.

*Did I have this same cashier last time? Does she recognize me? Why do I need to buy a 1.75 liter of*

*Maker's Mark at 10:30 in the morning on a Tuesday? Friday night after work made more sense.*

I tried validating my shopping with other groceries like I was shopping and planning for the week, making sure I mentioned the great deal buying two bottles of Absolute vodka while casually talking to the cashier.

I wanted to forget. I needed to forget − it was all too painful. Every minute was like a throbbing hour, a constant reminder of the failure I've become, screaming loud in my head with no escape, relief, or place to go. Like that old saying, wherever you go, there you are. There was no escaping myself...well, not in the way that quote represents. I just wanted not to think. Silence. Peace. Quiet existence. To slow the never-ending noise, chatter, condemnation, and the relentless beating and breaking of my own spirit. There was nothing left. I was nothing left - just a hollow shell of existence.

There were so many times I wanted and thought about going to the place of no return. It was only my kids that held me by a thread, a thin string of a will to live—not for me but for them. How could I be so selfish as to leave them with the mess of my memory? Taking the easy way out, leaving them to pick up the pieces and suffer the consequences of my life and robbing them of their own? It was the perfect recipe for years of counseling, seeking answers, releasing guilt, anger, and blame - wondering what they could have done differently or simply instilling the idea that they weren't enough.

I needed to cope, to run away from myself and the torture in my mind. I needed it to stop for me to be able to breathe and rest, like those few precious moments in between the agonizing contractions of giving birth. It was the temporary relief from it all.

## Blinked, A Poem by Thomas Christian Ward

And then I blinked. Reality washed over me again like a wave without warning, sending me spinning, disoriented, through the water that was my surroundings. I could feel the little bubbles of air as they rolled against my skin towards the surface, the voices echoing off of the inner walls of my head. Get out of my head. The reality was that I had slipped again. I never remember closing my eyes. Rushing me through doors, my bloodshot eyes stared above, watching the piercing fluorescent lights sprint past me like sick shooting stars, bathing the dirty walls in an electric white light. And then I blinked. No fluorescent white light but the comforting black I remember from behind my own eyelids. Inside, I am the Creator. The Rearranger. Free to dream infinite worlds just as I please. Outside, the Stranger. Chair-bound. Wrists rubbed raw from hopeless escape. The leather stiff, its cracked wrinkles curved into smiles laughing at me with the same amusement the others provided. The wheels screamed in agony and protested at each rotation, begging to rest.

Their voices shrill. The ringing. Get out of my head and then I blinked. A record danced around in empty space, its hunched back throwing the needle up and down like a bobbing ship at sea. Shuffling shoes grew louder, interrupting trumpets and cymbals and the resonating deepness of a standup bass. The baby blue pinstripes on her white pants gave the impression she was wearing pajamas, only further reinforced by the heelless white slippers that were general issue in the ward. Frizzy brown curls protruded from her head like Medusa's snakes with bright, piercing blue eyes that could just as easily cast you to stone. Their gaze paralyzing, stopping time and space itself, black pupils burned holes through my being, infecting me and spreading a curious darkness to my very core. She stood in front of my withered figure with the presence of God, with what I could imagine a demented mercy drawing her towards me like how one looks at an animal before sacrificial slaughter. The ringing. Chapped, pale lips began to part like the sea, her closed fists extending towards my chest holding something small. Silver. I recognize every pit, crack, and scratch on the pendant; we had one just like it. Get out of my head. I'm not crazy, I say, but even I begin to falter, swearing the sound I hear is her voice again. Those wrinkles that frame her face. Please, I'm so alone. I long for the past. I could dig my beating heart from my chest, just please don't leave. It's like I saw you yesterday, and then I blinked.

So incredibly talented with his artistic and symbolic writing. To me, it kind of represented my emotional state, when I felt like I was losing my mind.

## "I Know How You Feel"

Man, don't you hate when people say that? Seriously, they have no idea. I remember telling my live-in boyfriend, "There is no way you could go through and handle all that I have gone through." And he said, "You're right. I can't even imagine. I was off work and in transition for less than a week and crying on the couch like a baby."

Exactly! There is absolutely nothing worse than feeling completely lost and alone, wandering around with time moving so slow, thoughts continuously swirling around in your head of: *what am I doing? What can I do? Oh my Gosh, it's only 9:00 AM and I want to go back to bed.* You don't even know where to begin. Seriously, your whole life - identity, worth, reason for waking up in the morning - was for your career, your job, your business. And now, everything has stopped, except for the world around you. Everybody else has their daily routine, their agenda. They're off to work, following their schedules, kids, appointments, obligations, and opportunities; and here you are, still in your bathrobe wondering how you're going to spend the next eight hours of your day.

Gosh, if time only went this slow when you wanted it! You can barely even remember what it was like having a packed schedule and agenda.

Now, your day might look something like this:

*Let's see.... Should we watch Good Morning America? The View?*

*No, no, something motivational! Yes, some kind of CD, audio tape, recording, podcast... Oh my gosh, there are so many! What an awesome opportunity! It will be like taking a semester of class, specializing in (whatever). It's a total education in less than a week! This will surely get me going in the right direction!*

*Or, I could just go ahead and clean out my closet? I've been wanting to do that forever. Look at all these clothes I never wear anymore. Yeah, I can definitely give them away. That will make me feel good too.*

*Jeez, I've also never had time for a hobby. Look at all the things that I have never had the time to do: painting, crafts, ceramics, flower arranging, gardening – wow, all these opportunities!*

This is when you realize, there really isn't anything on TV during the day, and/or just trying keep yourself busy with mindless activities to help get you out of your slump and move you to purposeful action, just doesn't work if you're only trying to run away and keep your feelings pushed down.

You need to have the right mindset and intentions in doing them. It's so funny though, because when you're actually in your confident, unstoppable and unbreakable stature, you're fearless. You know nothing is impossible. You feel like you can take on the world and any adversity that may come along. Surely you can motivate yourself once again, right?

My past internal dialog has been: *Hello! Look at what you have accomplished. You are the bomb! So what? You'll just have to do it all over again tomorrow, but at least you have the skills and the know-how and the confidence to do it now. Right?"*

Wrong.

Nothing, I mean nothing, compares to losing your whole world, identity, self-esteem, worth, reason for waking up, or even the ability to give somebody eye contact without wanting to wither away. No, I don't even have the confidence to try to pretend to have confidence.

You're solid when you feel like you're living your truth or when there's nothing to hide. When you know without a shadow of a doubt, you are living, being, and doing all that you could be and more. You are living your highest path. There is so much energy and power in living your fullest capacity. It's easy to walk boldly, voice your opinion, and reach out to others because you feel you have something of value. You are on a path of making a difference and participating in changing the world. You know everything that you say and do comes from the heart, and you've got the Universe on your side. But when you're not in that emotional state or mindset, it's hard to do anything.

## That Was Then; This Is Now

Maybe you're not supposed to remember who you used to be. That's living and longing for the past - robbing, stealing, and consuming our present moment today and all the gifts that are awaiting us. If only we'd wake up and open our eyes to the now. The right here, in this moment of time...experiencing new thoughts and feelings, instead of trying to relive and yearn for yesterday; we would realize that there's so much more to us than what was. We're not over. It's not over. It isn't a movie that just ended. The story goes on and continues until our very last breath. We may ask ourselves: Is this a midlife crisis? Is this where everyone stops, ponders, analyzes, and overthinks everything from the past? How we wish things were different, and the regrets of what we did and did not do? Can we change it? No. But we can start now, again, fresh and new. We can create the life we still have, regardless of our age, to live out our dreams and move forward with new goals, for where we are right now. We can create new memories, ones that can and will make a difference to you and to others; not just still, silent memories of the past but something that lives on - a legacy that changes others and the world.

We have the opportunity while we are alive to love, create, explore, and be bold. I know there's so much more we can do and become. We limit ourselves with our preprogrammed and tarnished thinking and beliefs of what is possible. We do deserve a second chance at this game called life, to push past mistakes, forgive others, and most importantly, forgive ourselves. We have another chance to restore, do things we wished we had, and make up for the things that we did. We're still alive! At this very moment, we have a choice: live in the past with pain and sorrow or move forward until your time is up. Five minutes, five months, five years - we never know, do we? Just one step at a time, one day at a time. Write it down, and just do it. What things can you do and small changes can you make, that will allow you to live your life to the fullest? One that is true and authentic to yourself and not one others expect of you? A life you choose to and are brave enough to live? Small daily changes can have a powerful impact. Start with making a list of things outside of your own personal and immediate goals. For example, you can make a list of several senior citizen centers or assisted living facilities to go tour several times and interact with the residents. Find out what the standard schedule is like in addition to what some of the other special programs or activities that may be going on that month. Being able to visit and witness throughout the typical day, with eating, outside free time, bathing rituals, physical therapy, etc, really allows you to step outside your feeling-sorry-for-yourself program and into one of pure gratitude, realizing we are so blessed. What community activities or volunteer programs does your city have you could assist with or school programs that you can volunteer in? Or with the local library? We actually have a night every week where you can go and read to children. Seeing how inspired these children are while reading and giving them undivided attention, is extremely fulfilling and means so much to them as well. Again, it puts you in a different perspective and takes your eyes off yourself and lifts your heart to new levels. Being thankful, feeling blessed, looking at the lives of others and making a difference with helping, creates the energy levels and vibration it takes to move you past the low energy, negative vibrations that keep you stuck and inside your head.

Another thing I've done, which sounds extremely simple but yet impactful, was forcing myself to get in the car, out of the house, into a new environment, with new surroundings and playing loud music. I didn't have any place to go but just being out and about, seeing other people, the sky and the leaves on the trees changing color, lifted my spirit, which is sometimes all it takes to get you moving in the right direction. Other days, I would make a trip to the grocery store and make conversations with different people up-and-down the aisle and while standing in the checkout line. Gosh, I totally forgot how awesome it is and how much I love talking with people. It also makes their day too.

Chapter 4:

# Pull Over and
# Ask for Directions

believe what we all genuinely seek is that drive
and burning fire of desire to truly live for a cause,
a purpose of more than just financial accumulation.
There is a need to feel alive and strive toward a mission
that engulfs our hearts, deep within our souls, living
with intention and passion. There's a way of truly feeling instead of masking our emptiness and numbing the
emotions that tell us there's something more. We know
in our hearts this isn't all there is. We're falling short
of who we really are and living out our full potential -
emotionally, physically, and spiritually.

We either spend most of our time and existence
thinking and being outside of the now, wanting to

escape somewhere off in the visions of a future we believe will be the delivery of our happiness and fulfillment, or we're dwelling on the past. But in all reality, that day will never arrive because we're doing nothing but staying stuck. It shouldn't be at the end of our life, taking our last breath, that we finally realize that there are no more tomorrows or future to worry about. It's done and over with and we have wasted all of our minutes, buying into our own comfortable stories, allowing us to continue living small without risks and playing it safe for fear of failing again. It's such a waste when you think of the fact that you stopped living because you were afraid of what people thought about you, basing your self-identity and entire worth on their opinions. That's the problem with depending on external validation from people... including yourself.

I get it. I've done it for over a decade and I seriously can't believe it. It makes me so sad to think of all of the time I have wasted in my own head; time I have wasted being sad, depressed, feeling bad for myself and for everybody involved. All the time wasted being scared and not living up to my potential - the potential I knew I had, the potential I used to strive for every single day. While visiting senior assisted living centers and talking with residents, one of the top regrets that always came up when telling me their stories was wishing they had the courage to live their life true to themselves and not for the approval and expectations of others. Though it was very painful for several reasons, it was such a good experience and I recommend everyone, young and old, to do the same. It truly gives you an in-depth insight you could never otherwise obtain, unless on your own deathbed. Again, we can learn so much from others life experiences.

## Plan of Action

I believe if we really dissect our motivation on a day-to-day basis, we will see what it is we are truly seeking to get or striving to avoid. We live more out of fear than the pursuit of happiness. I want us to wake up, in every sense of the meaning - emotionally as well as literally - each and every day, to the excitement of living our gift. We are alive, and it is a gift. We are more than what we're expressing. What I truly yearn for you is to be aware and identify what it truly is that you desire in the end and ultimately work toward having it, with where you are and who you are right now.

If you are ready and want to live the life you've imagined it to be – the ultimate experience – then you need to look at each day as a fresh slate, another chance to do and be all that you can be instead of this continued thinking of your failure or past success. Your experiences could and would be completely different.

I truly believe if I had someone, something, a program, a system, other than the typical counseling (which gets you nowhere except with helping you regurgitate what you want to forget already and accept the hatred for the stellar one liner "How does that make you feel?"), I wouldn't have wasted thirteen years. I had already done my time, the legal consequences of what transpired, but I have remained in prison—my own prison, which has been a lot worse than being behind bars.

In jail, you don't have to make decisions; they're all made for you. There are rules and you follow them. You have no choice. And when you're dead inside, it doesn't really matter and actually, was kind of a good thing. You don't have to think.

*How much is enough?*

*How bad does it have to hurt?*

*How many times do you have to say you're sorry?*

*How long do you have to keep beating yourself before you feel worthy enough for a second chance to start over?*

*When do you finally get to forgive yourself?*

*How much time has to go by before you can feel good again, smiling, walking with your head up, interacting with others, having fun, laughing and feeling joyful?*

It's hard to do anything when you walk around with this black cloud surrounding you, feeling as though everyone knows and can see your past and, of course, judging you. This is true. At this point, I could have just walked around with a huge billboard sign plastered in the front and back of me saying "Total Loser and Here's Why".

My point is I want to offer you something different, something that can help you move on and finish what you came here for. More than likely if you're reading this book you were extremely successful – head of a department, organization or corporate job, or whatever you took pride in, loved, and considered your forever occupation and life. There is intense emotion and identity associated with it. How can there not be? It's what made us successful in the first place. It's why we feel we lost the biggest part of ourselves, or all of ourselves.

I want to help you get out of this self-sabotaging and internal prison. I know for sure it takes an enormous amount of support and understanding to move forward. Regardless of who you are and where you've been, we're all still people. We need community and connection in order to thrive or even survive for that matter. We need understanding and to know that we are heard. We need to feel safe and secure and have confidence in who we're with and what we disclose – the deepest part of ourselves.

Even now, after all these years and starting the next phase of my life, I still have to remind myself and my clients that not everybody deserves your pure and true heart; not everyone is entitled to know the most intimate and deepest part of you; not everybody is your best friend, so why treat them like they are? Being prepared with some simple scripts, depending on who you may run into or encounter, is definitely important in helping you to be able to start facing the public again with confidence. Having quick and ready answers for those who just want to know the scoop or for even those who really want to know how you're doing, makes all the difference. Either way, you'll have an easy answer that will come naturally, without stuttering or catching you off guard. This is something I can help you design and structure for the different scenarios and obviously depending upon your personality and your circumstance. The point is, to have something prepared for both the casual acquaintance and those who you have more of a relationship with.

In order to truly heal, we need to put ourselves first and foremost so that we can show up as our best selves for our family and for the ones we love. It serves nobody trying to hide, pretend, or cover up our insecurities with wanting to stay invisible. We certainly can't run from ourselves either.

# Chapter 5:

# Developing Your Vision

What's great about this?

It all starts with a vision. You need to release judgment and believe there is a new life for you. Even through all of the anguish and despair, I have surely seen miracles that I wouldn't have otherwise. I have experienced gifts and a deeper personal understanding that I wouldn't have been able to have seen or achieved while working the fast-paced lifestyle I once had. To the clients who were going through a divorce or losing their house or job, I would speak to them about how God and the universe has a plan even though we can't see it yet. I reminded them of how they've hated their job or that they knew their relationship wasn't going anywhere and it needed to be dissolved, so it was almost like He was giving you a helping nudge to get you into the right direction - almost like this idea of, *well if you're not going to do anything about it, let me help you out a little.*

Sometimes we wish and pray for something different, but we don't know where to even begin or what it is we truly want. We desire something to change, but we don't specify the exact route or even know how it's going to come about. Most of the time, we don't have a clue. We're unaware of things that we may have to go through to get to our next phase - and it's OK. This is where trust comes in—trust in a higher, all knowing power that is working on our behalf and in our favor. We just can't see it from this position. So, this is why it's so important to surrender and release all expectations you have on how you think the delivery is supposed to come. We have to trust, knowing that everything is happening for the highest good for all of us, again, looking at the big picture from the airplane versus the gravel road we're walking on.

I know for me it always takes hindsight and a look in the rearview mirror to discover blessings out of a tragedy or able to understand something that has taken place. Like the old saying goes, "Hindsight is 20/20."

This is exactly why I love to journal daily as well. It's so amazing to be able to look back on the situation and what you documented regarding how you were feeling, what you were doing, what time it was, any synchronicity and coincidences that have taken place, based on prayers, intention and being present and aware. This is where you see miracles unfold before your eyes. It gives us proof to believe in the beautiful tapestry of our lives.

There are so many times I've been able to share with people, the remarkable journal entry, where I wrote of something we were just discussing or what they're going through, like a personal message from above and I was the messenger. It still gives me chills and leaves me in awe about how wonderful it is that we're all connected-all one.

The goal here, though, is not to keep looking out that rearview mirror, the wake from the boat. That's why the front windshield is bigger and the boat is going in the other direction from the wake. We can learn from the past, yes, but the problem comes in when we spend too much time there dwelling, reminiscing, and regretting. We can definitely learn from our own past and that of others, but we need to move on and move forward as well. We need to live in the now so that we can have a better tomorrow, because how we live our lives matters and affects us, our family, our friends, and everyone we're in contact with.

There's so much more that goes on behind the scenes and what we see clearly on the surface. I know

now that I have been blessed through this tragedy of losing everything and realizing the gift of my intuition and being able to see the hearts of others. It's such an incredible opportunity for me to be able to connect, witness, and help others because I've been there and I'm willing to be vulnerable. It's selfish otherwise – a waste. Yes, it's scary exposing the deepest part of you, but it's such a wonderful gift when you risk in order to share with another. We help each other heal. I know exactly what it's like wanting to be able to think of the past without all the pain or wanting to throw up. It's difficult moving beyond the devastation and constant reminders of failure and humiliation; but using the experiences and lessons from the past to propel you forward and succeed even better than before is important, as well as trusting that it was all part of the bigger plan. I understand wanting to be able to live boldly again and out loud, excited to wake up and start the day, knowing all things are possible and miracles are just waiting to transpire.

I have gone to several three and five-day Tony Robbin functions and workshops - "Dates with Destiny," "The Power Within," etc. One of the main things he teaches first is that it is our emotional states that involve how we interpret everything around us, either through fear or love, or to avoid pain or seek pleasure.

I love his emphasis on how powerful words are, how just by changing the words we speak from a negative point of view to a positive one, changes everything. Asking the right questions is also so crucial. Instead of asking, "Why does this always happen to me? Why me?" Ask yourself, "What's great about this?" You can't help but to answer in a positive format. It's not asking, "Is there anything great?" It's asking, "What *is* great about this?" I had that quote for decades on my desk, as well as so many others, and it always made a difference. It makes you stop and really consciously seek out the good in everything and see from a different perspective.

## Goals: The Light

Use these steps and questions to help develop your own new life and strategic plan. If you don't have your own goals, somebody will use you for theirs.

- What is my next goal and the energy level I'm currently working with? Where do I need to be in order to achieve it?
- What little steps do I need to implement in order to move forward with a new life, business, career, or job? What is the first thing that would make the biggest difference in moving forward? The one thing that would make the biggest impact?

- Identify your strengths and your weaknesses. Write down what are you naturally good at or drawn to? This could be a good message for a path to explore that you may not have ever considered.

- Who's paying the price of me not doing this? People are waiting for you to get your stuff together, including yourself.

- Why are you stuck? What do you think the underlying reason is? Are you scared, unsure? Afraid of failure? Yes, there's change and uncertainty with anything new. Feel the fear and do it anyway.

- And how? Are you loosing self-esteem and motivation with waiting or denying what you need to do?

- Where are you paying the price? Think of all the painful consequences and lost opportunities by staying where you are. Really imagine all that it entails and how it will affect you, your loved ones and future.

- What benefits are you getting from staying stuck? Comfort of not risking anything? Not having to step up to do or face anything? You're getting something by staying there.

- Create urgency. Life is ticking by. Set beginning and end dates to activate and achieve what you want. Theres also real magic with writing it all down. Just do it. Start small and simple. It will help you feel productive when you start moving in the right direction and see where you're going.

- Time is our most valuable asset. We are the average of the five people we surround ourselves with. We're either going up or down, forward or backward, so why do we spend it working with or being around people who don't envision the long-term future together? Who's going to help support and pull you up?

- I want to go through this journey with you, building a relationship you can count on, someone who knows and cares and can provide you with the resources to keep going. I believe it's my calling—you didn't go through all you went through for nothing and neither did I. A partnership and true accountability was the single most important aspect for me in moving out of my depression and building up the confidence I needed to try again.

- I have learned that it is your secret that is your poison. Stop thinking and believing you have to live with it or that you're being punished as I did. Expose it, dig it out, and release it.

- Slowly but surely, we are killing ourselves. It's not the others we want to accuse or blame for our regression but ourselves. Forgive yourself; be kind. I think of my daughter, knowing that I would never treat or speak to her the way I treat and speak to myself. Write yourself a love letter, for not forgiving or moving past the memories and trauma...for the story we keep alive in our minds. It is us that keeps us stuck in the past, even more than the others we allow to. Leave yourself little notes of affirmations throughout your house, on the mirrors and in your car or wherever can see them every day. Even if you don't currently believe them (it's difficult when you first start out) with practice and consistency every day, it will become easier and they will become your new beliefs.

- Stepping up and into your fear and exposing the thing that you're most afraid of, will literally set you free. Picture others forgiving you, seeing your innocence. See yourself forgiving others and see yourself free.

- When we shine light into the darkness, there is no more darkness—only light. There is no hiding. It's all exposed with the light. As for your miracles, set your intentions. Feel free to use one of my favorite affirmations that I wrote (or go deep inside yourself) after reading and meditating. Just start writing with feeling. That's the magic part of the law of attraction.

## Dear Lord Spirit: One of my favorite affirmations I wrote

Dear Lord, Spirit, all that came before me, all that are gone physically, Universe, love, life, creator, force, all-knowing presence, living energy, sweet disguised angels everywhere I see, fill my heart, soul and mind with goodness, hope, faith, love for everyone, everything.

Help me see your presence, miracles, and power, every day, every hour, every minute. Fill me with peace, comfort, and the knowing you always conspire for me, bringing me joy as you show me proof even in the little things.

You are alive and everywhere. We are a tiny piece of you living an experience in this physical body, on this little ball called Earth. There is so, so, so much more than what this human mind can conceive...like we are that little five-year-old that doesn't know anything but the reality of what they're living, seeing, doing, feeling. Today, right now, is all they know. Pure innocence, amazed with exploration because everything is new, everything is exciting, and their energy is everlasting, never wanting to sleep for fear of missing a single thing.

Help me be that little child, knowing only the joy of always being in the present moment, never preoccupied with what the future may or may not hold, regretting the past and mistakes, worrying about tomorrow and the inability to forgive themselves, myself, for what is perceived to be shortcomings and less than perfect in the eyes that have been blinded with pictures of what's been portrayed to be truth. The stories told and the lies that fill our minds, competing for our attention, striving to be the focal point of our existence.

Help me to remember who I am, what I am, and the magnificent power that lies within me, around me, and through me.

Help me to recall all of the miracles since the Universe existed and before, that there is nothing left to prove, nothing to judge, fix, transform, or change. Only to Be, to allow and relish in the right here, right now, expressing love from within, through every cell and pore of my being. Command the same from everyone, everything, wherever I am and even where I am not, through the power of my intention. Thank you.

## Other Affirmations after my sentence

I have won the lottery. I hold the winning ticket in my hands. I turn it in and redeem the ultimate grand prize. I am joyful and happy with excitement and anticipation as I play and have fun every single day. Just when I think I've seen and done it all, I am whisked away to another level of euphoria. I love all my gifts and surprises. I am lavishly spoiled. My heart is always grateful as I experience every sense of pleasure, every minute, of every hour, of every single day. I'm excited every morning to wake up and do it all over again. Thank you.

We are here for a reason, a purpose that we can't even see. That's where faith comes in—period—the ability to keep moving forward regardless.

Always set your goals and affirmations in the present tense, already done and accomplished.

## Leesa's Affirmation: Thursday July 10th, 2014

My magical influence is like sparkling fairy dust, iridescent glitter that sticks to everyone and everything. I build rapport easily, gaining trust as others are able to see my heart and sincerity. People, animals, and even what may seem to be nonliving, are attracted to me like a strong magnet. I connect with people and circumstances that align with my goals and vision, thus building a bigger network of affiliates, which is always expanding with even more opportunities. I am awake and with an open heart. I see clearly all that is in front of me and beyond. I make decisions quickly and easily because it's so obvious, and I continuously hear God's voice. I always trust my intuition, which goes beyond my five other senses, knowing its accuracy in directing my paths and the way I should go. Like a compass, a detailed map, and a well-lit road, I move forward with total confidence and without hesitation. My energy fuels itself and continues to build like a rolling snowball down a steep mountain. Just as the universe responds to gravity without question, it responds to all of my requests, giving me the resources to do and be all that I came here for. I know I'm alive to do something big, to make a difference, and to help wake others up to want to do the same. I am excited every morning with anticipation as if I were opening Christmas presents, each one wrapped beautifully. And as I enjoy the process of removing the layers that conceal the special gift that someone has so lovingly given me and all that it means, my heart is touched, and I accept the gift. Thank you.

## Ebb and Flow

Pray specifically. Ask right questions for the deep meaning. Do something and take action. Everybody else is doing their part. Don't be the passive victim. Surrender, trust intuition, and go with the flow. Want but not with a specific delivery. Be open, it may come another way. Breathe, accept, allow, and trust the unfolding the plan.

Do you feel hesitation or maybe question if it's the right choice? Your voice is your most powerful sound; speak intentions out loud. You're the co-creator with the Universe who is behind you. So speak with conviction. Hesitation equals you being the victim. Don't fight against change. Just tune in. Be awake and acknowledge all things are in divine order. Ebb has a great value. Study what it's asking you to release, change, and move on. It's a signal and a sign that you're ready to move up to the next grade- a.k.a, the beautiful fable, The Lesson, by Caroline Pearson.

Resisting is the longest stage. Quiet our reactions and go inward and listen. Creatively respond to the change.

- What cycle are you in now? Ebb or flow?
- What does your spirit want to let go? Release? Surrender?
- What are some unexpected challenges? In what ways could they be inviting you to grow or expand your vision?
- Are you clinging to old beliefs or aspects of yourself that no longer serve you?
- How does holding onto rather than letting go of and growing, make you feel?
- Do you find yourself forgetting you're a divine being and more like a victim?

- What gifts or talents have you discovered in yourself? Remember, resisting is the longest stage.

## Death

Death equals more than just the physical we all define it to be. When you lose something, anything you love, it's death. Some put more importance on what they believe is valid enough to mourn and can't or don't understand when someone is devastated with the loss of something like a career or life work/position. When you put the value of your life, yourself, with what you do, it's devastating, and death has occurred—the death of who we thought we were. Yes, I know it's ego. We're sad for the person we once were. She's gone and you miss her like losing your best friend. There's a real emptiness that can't be filled because that was all you knew, all you ever wanted, it was your life. I get it. I feel like I had lost everything except for my physical body; I was forced to try and function in its existence. It made me question everything I believed was true with complete conviction. Like all mourning processes, you start with denial, then anger, bargaining, depression, and then finally acceptance. It's part of the framework that makes up our learning to live with what we've lost, whether it's a job, relationships, a home, possessions, or security.

Chapter 6:

# Expect Delays

## Make a List of What you Love

It's so important to be prepared. When you're in love, happy, and free flowing, things seem easy and obvious. However, when you are in the dark-despair-sad-hopeless state, it's hard to even think what could help you get out of it. I have found going into bookstores and searching self-help and spiritual titles and just being in that environment, helps me to feel grounded again. Other things that make me feel good, are doing something exciting or unexpected. Creating something from nothing out of everyday items, or recycling. I love crafts – decorating, visualizing, and being in nature with animals. I love music, dancing, or working on something emotional. Try making someone else's day happy, making somebody laugh, or connecting on a real level. It will brighten your day and wake others up. I truly feel, if we all worked together with love, instead of competing, we could all live in a wonderful and fulfilling world with joy and enthusiasm.

Other things I like to focus on, are letting others know that I love them – writing a little note, making gifts and giving to others. It is so awesome and feels so good doing something unexpected for someone. Also, sitting next to somebody that is present. Being around authentic individuals who can carry on a deeper conversation versus a superficial one, learning what they do, who they are, lessons they've learned, and how they live their life. Get to know their inner being. Their true story not the facade. What's their favorite author, movie, love, experience? What makes them alive? And notice how you feel and learn about yourself because of what they tell you. How can you interact or touch them? What can you contribute, even on this very small and broken level?

Once, I was talking to a woman I met at a glass company Christmas dinner. We spoke of our families and how difficult it is being a mom and having a full-time career without feeling guilty. I told her about each of my kids' journals - something so simple and that came easily for me, made a big difference to her. She was excited to start implementing what I told her I did, to feel more connected to her kids, with writing and leaving them love letters to read in the future. Loving people can be inspiring and so motivating...I've made a difference and I know that we all want the same thing, to be able to be present, naked and giving them permission to do the same without the typical front.

Write a list out when you're happy of all of the things that make you happy and the people you can connect with so when you aren't, you can read it, giving you a helping hand to guide yourself into a higher vibration. Expect delays, setbacks, and potholes in the road. Arm yourself with tools that keep you moving forward.

## Going Through a Tragedy

When you're going through a tragedy or some life-changing event, it's hard to get through it alone - especially when it involves humiliation and shame. It's pretty deep and personal, and I believe you need a true support system, people, accountability, accessibility, understanding, and care that can help you move past all of the daily obstacles, insecurities, giving you the ability to feel safe and loved.

## Tools and the How-To Manual on Supporting People

I have found that you can't really depend on your friends and family, not because they don't care, but because they just don't care. I'm joking. But seriously, the truth is, we all have our own lives and responsibilities...full of obligations with work, spouses, kids, school activities, and all the other countless, outside expectations and commitments. Life is full and cram-packed. And even though they do love and care about you, they've never been in your shoes, having to deal with what they think you should already be over by now.

Lots of people love giving you advice and telling you what to do and how to fix your problems. Most have good intentions, but the truth is, there really isn't anything they can do. It's an inside job, and it's up to us. It's a process, a journey, and takes time and a lot of soul-searching and inner work to heal. It's just nice to know that someone is there and has your back.

People want you to move on because there is nothing else they can do or say... because it makes them feel uncomfortable. Your relationships get strained, sometimes you're not sure what to talk about. You start to feel like you need to conceal that you're still hurting. You put up a front just to get through the interaction, which leaves you feeling even more lonely, empty, and disconnected.

Just as it is when a death has occurred, you're surrounded by people—friends, family, associates—and everybody acknowledges your loss. Funeral cards, flowers, reception stories, pictures, and even days after the funeral, neighbors and family continue to bring you casseroles and ask if there's anything that you need. Then slowly but surely, it trickles down to a few calls, asking again if there's anything you need. Then you're alone, while everyone else is off living their hustled life and going back to their fast-paced, daily routines.

That's exactly how it is going through what you're going through, and what I went through for over a decade—alone, lost, unsure, scared, stomach in a constant turn, and nonstop crying. Seriously, I've never cried so much, even adding up all the years of my entire life.

I kept thinking tomorrow is going to be different, but then I'd wake up once again only to wish that I just wouldn't anymore. I was finally at the point with my mind racing nonstop on ways I didn't have to do this anymore. Not one more day. I truly understood how people could take their own life—not that they didn't necessarily want to live, but they just didn't want to feel the intense pain that they felt like would never end. If it wasn't for my kids, I would have left this world. I also started to understand so many other self-sabotaging habits and behavioral issues others have adopted in order to deal with their pain. For example, like cutting. Not that I engaged in it, but there's just a lot of things you start thinking about that never would have even crossed your mind if you weren't feeling so low. I believe it's because you want to mask the internal pain, or at least to make the outside hurt as much as the inside - to see evidence of how or what you're feeling. Well, that's just my analogy anyway. I know I wanted to do anything that I thought would just make it all stop.

## The Struggle for Perfection, Approval, and Acceptance

The strive for perfection, approval, and smile of others. Acceptance, love and forgiveness.

Please, just walk in my shoes, really. So much judgment and the torment of feeling it all. Am I now in the world I never knew?

I've stepped outside my life, and now, I am a soul observer. Constant reflection, always thinking. Life, and everyone in it, seems to be in slow motion. When I drive, sometimes it feels way too fast, like I can't possibly look at everything off the street; buildings, business signs, people walking, stop lights, cross walks - so much commotion taking place all at once; slow and fast. I feel like I'm somewhere foreign, out of place, afraid with so much uncertainty. I wonder if this is how a panic attack feels like.

# Chapter 7:

# Repairing Relationships with Loved Ones

After my humiliation and in the aftermath of it, even though I was supposedly "free," there was still so much torture, shame, guilt, and punishment I felt I deserved, along with the constant reminder of everything I have done that had an impact on somebody's life.

Just because the legal consequences and trials and judgments are over with, doesn't mean that the pain, torture, and aftermath doesn't continue long after. How do you continue or even try to rebuild a relationship with somebody you knew you affected? After you changed the course of their life? Family get-togethers are hardly the same. What do you talk about? How do you not think and remember all that has transpired? How do you talk about what's new?

"What do you have planned? Where do you see yourself in five years?"

Oh wait...

Yeah, that's where I come in.

Even when you're forgiven, it never really, really goes away. Does it? No. You remember. They remember. It never goes away; the ramifications will be lifelong. There's no amount of apology, no amount of trying to make it up. There is no amount of trying to do something "special" to outweigh the sting and memory of the bad. It is what it is—done. There's no sugar-coating, and nobody is all of a sudden going to forget the bad and look at the good, regardless of whatever you do.

Confronting head-on and facing what has transpired with the people you care about and love (and with even those you may not so much) helps jumpstart the healing and process of moving forward. - even without their consent, approval, or forgiveness. You need to do this for you, for "closure" or at least for a stepping-stone to move forward.

Write yourself a letter, the way you would to the most important person in your life - with love and gentleness - giving yourself permission to move forward without all of the baggage you've been carrying for so long. Forgive yourself, the way you would hope others would, knowing you did the best you could and without ill will or gains.

Write a letter to each person you may have offended or to the circumstances, as an entity, that have led you to where you are right now. Explain all of the details from your perspective and acknowledge their position and how they may be feeling. Imagine loving exchanges. Meditate on the closure of it all.

If you're an intuitive and an over-the-top empath, this is so extremely important for you. Obviously if you are reading this book and you've gotten this far, you are like me in that you want everyone to be happy and feel good, including yourself.

It's frustrating that sometimes you just can't control the outcome of your efforts like you'd hope for, but that's really not the point. Yes, this is another lesson we need to deal with all on our own. It goes back to release and surrender.

It's the same when people would ask me why I am giving the money to the homeless or whoever standing at the corner. "They're only going to buy drugs or alcohol." Yeah, maybe, and that's up to them. It's not up to me to say what they can or cannot buy with what I am giving to them. That shouldn't make a difference. Give without expectation. You give without any contingency. You do your part, and the rest is up to the other person to do whatever they want. I just think people use this as an excuse, some kind of justification to not feel bad about not giving to someone in need or a specific cause. But it all goes back to you just doing your part. You can only control you and your part. And that is enough.

*"The reason you are here is not to be good, to be perfect, to get 'stuff' done, to save the world, to save somebody, to prove something, or to be anything other than yourself. That's all you have to work on. That's all you can do. But by doing it, all those other things will happen anyway."–* Mike Dooley, *Notes from the Universe.*

In addition to all of the required and continued education courses for real estate agents, brokers, and the like, we also take advantage of other courses, workshops, and speakers to assist with marketing, business ideas, and new implementations. Everybody has their niche, but regardless, most of the time I thought to myself *Yeah, OK, I know and am familiar with this, but I also know, if you can walk away with just one new thing, even just ten percent more than what you knew or was being implemented, it was so worth the time and money invested.*

One such trainer, Joe Stumpt, specialized in relationships. He worked his whole course and program around a system he called "By Referral Only." Essentially his message said this: instead of trying to spend money advertising and generating/ chasing new leads, focus on taking care of the ones you have and the past clients that you've built relationships with, and that will more than likely be selling and moving up purchasing another.

That was great and all, but I've been busting my butt in this fast-paced, do-or-die business, and now it's been five years since I've spoken to any of my original clients. How are you supposed to re-engage and connect when there's been so much time in between?

## Speaking Truth from the Heart

Scary? Intimidating? Yes.

I was basically opening a door to condemnation, criticizing, and judgment by sending out a letter to everyone I had ever worked with, trying to touch base and reconnect. I started with thanking them for the opportunity I had with working with them with the biggest and most important investment of their lifetime. They gave me the ultimate trust to take care of them financially and their family, goals, kids, lifestyle, etc.

I then apologized. I apologized for not keeping in touch, for not following up, for not making sure everything was OK. I never wanted our relationship to feel like a one-night stand. And if it was me on the other side, I might feel that way.

I also outright and humbly asked what was something I could have done differently before, during, or after their purchase or sale of their home, that would have made a difference -whether by making it easier, more meaningful, making them feel more taken care of, special, important, secure, safe—whatever would earn me the right of being able to work with them again. I sincerely wanted their feedback, and I only wanted to improve the service I provided. I asked if there was anything else they could tell me, I would be so appreciative.

The responses were similar and surprisingly nice. I was actually dreading what might come back. The one thing I remember was the fact that most thought it was bold of me to reach out and ask for sincere feedback, criticism, and ways to improve my business. It was appreciated that I would go out of my way, even at the expense of negativity, to ensure I would provide the best service possible and to change anything that would make a difference in the future.

I tell you this because it helps with starting fresh. Regardless of the circumstances, when you can meet whatever and whoever, with where they're at, it's out in the open. You've done your part. You've confronted it. You were there to address, conclude, and move forward from that place in the past, even if only for yourself.

You can do this with what you're going through now, regardless of the reciprocation or if there's any forgivingness. You know you did your part. You know you did all you could putting it out there regardless of the repercussions or consequences. You reached out. You may or may not have tried to make amends, but regardless, you came forward offering your truth and vulnerability. You created the space for open communication and resolving past issues or misunderstandings.

## Trust Your Instincts, Question Your Habits

Sometimes it feels like sleepwalking with a collection of good memories (over-glorified, exaggerated bliss) or bad memories (terrorized, victim-blaming today for yesterday). Most of the time, we go through activities day-by-day, not really living but just existing without conscious, purposeful attention. We are a slave to distraction. It will take some catastrophe, some major occurrence, death, or a near death of ourselves, to finally wake up and snap us out of the past and start reengaging in the now, like an intervention from and to yourself.

Same goes for always thinking about the future. Worry and anxiety about hardships, what's in store, or even wishing and daydreaming, can steal our joy in the present moment and living today. Any of the above can be used as another way to escape, being here. If you're not now-here, you are no-where.

One of my all-time favorite movies is *The Peaceful Warrior* with Nick Nolte. It's such a beautiful story that demonstrates how we live through our ego and hide behind the masks to keep us safe, therefore missing what is real and in front of us. We miss all the beautiful, little insignificant treasures throughout the day and interacting with others.

Every time I watch it, I gain new insight. There are several good messages throughout. It was such an emotional movie for me because the young gymnast who was on top of his game had everything he wanted − looks, girls, status, top competitor. Basically, total swag. Then, he shattered his legs in a motorcycle accident and could no longer compete in the Olympics he worked so hard for his entire life. He felt like he lost his whole life, his whole meaning and purpose, all of his goals and the future gone. Even though he was still in college, he felt like his life was over. This was the only thing he lived for, the only thing that made him feel powerful and the only thing he could see himself doing. Like me, there was no plan B.

The movie continues to show how he discovers his true self and how to be in the present moment; how to be aware of your thoughts and actions, and not live out of default. It's very entertaining in addition to the core message and all the lessons it provides.

## Lessons from Books

The majority of the books I read and the movies I watch, are some sort of self-help or motivational life lesson in how to better myself. That's not to say they are always an A through Z, steps one through ten book. Sometimes, the best lessons and comprehension of them, is through stories. My favorite, favorite, favorite book is *The Monk Who Sold His Ferrari* by Robin Sharma. It's about a high-powered attorney who collapses and is forced to reevaluate his life, and we get to go through the journey with him. Again, it's about being in the present moment, stopping to smell the roses, etc. It's a perfect combination of Deepak Chopra and Tony Robbins. I love it! Ok, and just a quick plug for Andy Andrews - his books are awesome, like *The Noticer* and *The Traveler's Gift*.

> *Experience is a hard teacher because she gives the test first, the lesson afterward...*
> —Vernon Law

We are the sum of what we read, watch and who we hang around. We need to make sure that we surround ourselves with positive influences that support our life choices, that build us up and keep us grounded and moving in the direction of our goals. When you think about the fact that three percent of the population is "successful"—and not within the norm of society's standards—we need to make sure to guard ourselves from the influences that may slowly creep into our thinking and affect our habits.

## Power Versus Force

Doctor David R. Hawkins also discusses in his book *Power vs. Force,* the different levels of human consciousness. He has simplified it in a form of points from twenty equaling shame to 1000 for total enlightenment, the highest state, in order to demonstrate and describe the emotional correlation of the energy that we carry and therefore manifest into our state of being.

This is the starting point which affects everything in life and the perception of ourselves, which creates a lens/filter in the way we view the world around us and everyone in it. Obviously, this affects everything in our life, from the way we interact with other people, if we do at all, and how we feel about ourselves, which trickles down over all things.

For an in-depth and thorough understanding, you would definitely have to buy his book. I'm barely qualified to try and interpret all of the scientific jargon, but

I wanted to show in terms of the levels and how devastating shame and humiliation is.

The fact that you and I are alive and that you are now reading this book, means we are in the top percentile that have forged our way through this pain enough to want to work at improving ourselves and getting out of this depressive rut to move forward.

## Energy Level Twenty — Shame

The level of shame is perilously proximate to death. It's more than just feeling the pain of "losing face," becoming discredited or feeling like a non-person. In shame, we hang our heads and slink away, wishing we were invisible. Death by conscious suicide or avoidable accident is common here.

## Energy Level Thirty — Guilt

Guilt is often used in our society to manipulate and punish, which manifests itself in a variety of expressions such as remorse, self-recrimination, and masochism, and the whole gamut of symptoms of victimhood. Unconscious guilt also results in accident proneness and suicidal behaviors.

## Energy Level Fifty — Apathy

This level is characterized by poverty, despair, and hopelessness. The world and the future look bleak.

Apathy is a state of helplessness, its victims, needy in every way, lack resources, energy to avail themselves of what may be available, and less external energy is supplied by caregivers. Death through passive suicide can result without the will to live, hopeless, staring blankly, unresponsive to stimuli until their eyes stopped tracking, and there isn't enough energy left to even swallow offered food. Apathy is the level of abandonment of hope, and few have the courage to really look in its face.

## Energy Level Seventy-Five — Grief

This is the level of sadness, loss, and dependency. Most of us have experienced it for periods of time, but those who remain at this level, live a life of constant regret and depression. This is the level of mourning, bereavement, and remorse about the past. It's also the level of habitual "losers" who accept failure as part of their lifestyle, often resulting in loss of jobs, friends, family, and opportunity, as well as money and health. In grief, one sees sadness everywhere—in little children and in life itself. This level colors one's entire vision of existence, irreplaceability of what's been lost or that which it symbolizes. At this level, such emotional losses may trigger a serious depression or death. Grief is the cemetery of life.

## Energy Level One Hundred — Fear

From the viewpoint of this level, the world looks hazardous, full of traps and threats. Fear is the favored official tool for control in advertising, market shares, and world news. Play to fear to increase market shares. Once fear is one's focus, the endless worrisome events of the world continue to feed it. Fear becomes an obsession and may take on any form including losing relationships to jealousy, chronically high stress; fearful thinking can balloon into paranoia or generate neurotic defensive structures and, because it's contagious, become a dominant social trend. Fear limits growth of the personality and leads to inhibition. It takes energy to rise above fear. The oppressed are unable to reach a higher level unaided. Fearful seek strong leaders who appear to have conquered their own fears.

And the book goes on to describe the other energy levels – Desire 125, Anger 150, Pride 175 (and not the good kind), Courage 200, Neutrality 250, Willingness 310, Acceptance 350, Reason 400, Love 500, Joy 540, Peace 600, and finally Enlightenment with levels of 700 to 1000.

## Patanjali: Inspiration

One of my most favorite quotes comes from the great spiritual teacher Patanjali. "When you are inspired by some great purpose, some extraordinary project, all your thoughts break their bonds. Your mind transcends limitations. Your consciousness expands in every direction. And you find yourself in a new, great, and wonderful world.

"Dormant forces, faculties, and talents become alive, and you discover yourself to be a greater person by far than you ever dreamed yourself to be."

Imagine that just by moving into the world of inspiration, you can activate "dormant forces," forces you thought were dead, that you thought were not available to you. You can make them work for you when you are inspired. You don't get tired. You don't get hungry. You don't worry about money, and you don't worry about what's going to happen tomorrow. You're moving into the world of God, our energy source of all things.

Being inspired is probably one of the most important things you can do. Look at all the things around you and ask, "Where did all this come from?" It came from the world of spirit, the world of being in-spirit—inspiration.

It is so important to feel inspired with a purpose, a purpose for living, contributing, being of value. When it flows and is as easy as breathing, then you know you found your passion. It's amazing how much energy comes with being passionate. Everything is brighter, stars twinkle, everything's happier and full of love - smiles, birds, flowers, floating butterflies, children laughing, sun shining, moon glowing, flowing water, music from neighbors having a barbecue, dancing leaves on trees and bushes, a gentle breeze. Everything is alive. The plants talk to me. And I know they feel my presence. I give them love. Pieces of wood and broken logs speak of their past lives, all who've benefited from their existence—animals' homes, humans' shade and shelter; rocks penetrate their energy when I hold them. There's life in everything.

Being conscious, aware, and present, allows you to capture those moments of joy and pieces of bliss, giving you a glimpse into what your soul and what your true self and intuition is telling you − a gentle suggestion, whispering to your heart, leading you into the direction of your true desire and a new change from what you think you should be doing. Be open.

This is the real you, the you that knows there is more than just making a living and working a job for recognition and status. The real you - the one who doesn't need to feel important, accepted, following the rules and expectations from others. You are able to proudly state what you do when others ask. So, when you really think about it, ask yourself who you are really living for based on the above. The majority or the norm is not for you but for others. Follow the path that is your own.

Now, here you are, slowed down enough to really see, ponder, reanalyze, and start fresh, once and for all. You'll see all of this has really been a blessing in disguise.

## Reticular Activating System

I've always been intrigued by psychology, quantum physics and the like, looking in depth of how our brains work- how we are so unaware of its magnificent power and what goes on behind the scenes. For example, the reticular activating system is a bundle of nerves at our brainstem, that filters out the unnecessary information, so the important stuff gets through. It is the main reason you learn a new word, for example, and then start hearing it everywhere you go. You can literally change the way you look and perceive the world around you.

If you care about positivity, for example, you will become more aware of and seek positivity. If you really want a pet chicken and set your intention on getting one, you'll tune in to the right information that helps you do that. When you look at it this way, the law of attraction doesn't seem so mystical. Focus on the bad things, and you will invite negativity into your life. Focus on the good things, and they will come to you because your brain is seeking them out. It's not magic; it's your reticular activating system influencing the world you see around you. Our brains look out for our best interests. Our RAS is filtering through billions of pieces of data so we can see, hear, and be what we want to be. It's not out of our control, though. It can also be trained. It's about visualizing what we want and then letting our subconscious and conscious work together to make it happen.

Do an experiment. Make a decision to notice all the green cars on the road or how many people are wearing hats or walking dogs. I'd ask questions through my prayer/meditation for the universe to speak to me through whatever I experienced that day - a word spoken, a billboard or a message for me, connecting with a stranger, or any other way etc.

There are answers all around us. Be open. Sometimes we need to realize it's not coming in the form we're used to. It's more like a crossword puzzle, a treasure hunt, or one of those pictures that takes a minute to see beyond the obvious. Behind the background, within the trees, we can see the wolf. We need to put on our 3-D glasses and get the depths of what our spirit is communicating to us.

There is so much more to say, so many people and situations and circumstances that I have not included in this book because mainly it's not about that. It's not about my story. And it wouldn't be fair to tell anyone else either. Everyone has their own perception depending on which part of the elephant they were touching. It's about you and helping you to move on so that you don't waste another single day of your life in the past.

I like to think about things like, how many more summers do you have left? How many more days to be in a bathing suit, to go swimming, to be on the beach and have picnics? How many more winters do you have that you're able to go skiing? Have hot chocolate in front of a fireplace? When you break it down to that simplicity of seasons, it's so much shorter than what you're thinking...that you have plenty of time-the rest of your life in front of you, but what if it's only for another week?

Chapter 8:

# Have Faith

F irst and foremost, I'm in no way wanting to insult, persuade, or push any of my personal thoughts, opinions or beliefs on you. We all have what resonates what truth is for us. I have learned and experienced so much, as I'm sure we all have, with continuing to evolve. I only want to share my background, where I was and where I am today, when it comes to faith, spirituality and "religion" in order to give you a glimpse of who I was and how I strove to live daily. It's what I believe has been a lesson within a lesson. It has been such a huge part of my life—both good and bad—so there is just no way around not including it.

I felt like I was always directed by Divine Intervention – walking as one with God. I raised my kids that way. They went to a Christian school and attended regular bible studies. I also expressed it in my office and witnessed to my clients the same way, wanting to give hope and express sincere love. There is so much energy and power when living your fullest capacity. It's easy to walk boldly, to voice your opinion, to want to reach out to share with others because you feel you have something of value. You know that everything you say and do comes from the heart and you've got the Universe on your side. I truly felt all things were possible and that I was completely, one hundred percent protected because I was living truthfully and was in God's favor.

*"If God is for us, who can be against us?"* – Romans 8:31, New International Version.

*"I have learned to be content whatever the circumstances. I know what it is to be in need, and I know what it is to have plenty. I have learned the secret of being content in any and every situation. "I can do all things through Christ who strengthens me"* – Philippians 4:11-13, New King James Version.

If you've picked up this book, it is not by accident. It is not by coincidence. It is all Divine Intervention or with whatever you believe…God, Spirit, Source, the Universe - it's all the same thing. It's only when you're wrapped up and tied into a religious network, that it's hard to open your mind to what *is* all around you. All the different religious, institutions and denominations, want you to believe *their* way is the only way.

We are all sadly so separated *due* to religion - the thing that is supposed to connect us as one and show love and light through what we believe in. The thing that is supposed to express unconditional love, compassion, understanding, and the desire to help your fellow brother or sister. The old saying "actions speak louder than words" is so apparently true and so obvious in times like these.

I used to drive around in my brand-new Mercedes and Lexus with a fish emblem on the back and my license plate saying, "With Jesus all things are possible." I wanted to make a statement, a bold statement, representing my faith because all I'd ever seen was a barely running, smoking Pinto with a "Jesus is the answer" sticker on the bumper. But then, we really shouldn't have to advertise it, should we? It should be evident by the way we live, act, and treat each other.

I wanted to demonstrate that you could be successful *and* have faith. It's the one thing that got me in to church in the first place - seeing my mentor Vina driving a light blue Mercedes in and out of the church parking lot. I was like, "Wow, you don't have to be a martyr, living in the streets, with a can, collecting left-over change to believe in God. And wow! She's even wearing makeup and a cool outfit!"

I was invited to go to church with my sister Maria when we got a ride on the way back from a party in August 1987. We went up to the altar and were baptized that same month. Since then, my whole life and purpose was to be "a good girl", to make God happy with my choices and the fact that I wanted to follow Him. I was obsessed. I literally read the Bible for hours a day, learning all the different books and memorizing scripture. At that point, I was so convinced, I wasn't even scared if I got into a car accident because I knew I was "saved" and would be going to Heaven.

The problem with believing in Heaven and Hell is when you're not living up to what you *think* you should be, it's torturous, or when you contemplate suicide, as I have several times, it kind of stops you. I didn't want to go to hell forever. I was already living in it.

You start buying into the whole sin thing (which I never could even stand seeing the word sin) and never feel worthy enough for anything or anybody. It's a sick joke. Fear and punishment have never been a motivating factor for me. I've read all the scripture in all the different formats: *King James, Living Bible, Christian Contemporary, New American Standard, New International Version, and the One Year Bible,* in addition to other Bible studies with Mormons and Jehovah Witnesses. Every religion has their own rules, morals, purpose, focus, and emphasis on why they're different from everybody else. It's like a competition within the whole religious sector. Again, embarrassing. How do you even stick up for that?

Why compete if the main goal is to show the love of Christ, his example, and to help people to experience unconditional love? If that's the goal, then why are we fighting about it? Why is there so much anger and hate? Why is it so confusing? Seriously, do you really think God, the Universe, the Almighty maker of everything, wants *this*? There are many teachers besides Jesus Christ. We're all witnesses. We're all so busy and wrapped up in trying to prove each other wrong, fighting for our stance, making a point, that we forget the whole objective and mission in the first place. Seriously, when you really step back and look at it, it's so obvious and pretty embarrassing. Really embarrassing. No wonder so many have fled or avoid anything to do with church or organized religion. "God" is kind of taboo, and more and more people choose to use other words and different titles to define their belief in a higher power.

*You are not a body with a soul but rather a soul with a body, not a human being having a spiritual experience but a spiritual being having and living a human experience.*

## Perception Is Everything

I don't know where I got it, but I have this extreme anger towards men and for the rights of women. How could that be when I have been a shy little girl my whole life until high school? I never had an opinion or stood up for anything. It's also the main thing that drove me in my business to compete, be successful, and the reason I would boldly voice my opinions.

Or maybe it was just because I have been kept silent for so many years. My dad was married and had several girlfriends, including my mom. He had three children with her, while he was still married.

Maybe it's because of everything that I saw growing up as a girl. Men, boys, uncles, dads, cousins – they don't miss an opportunity to take advantage of you. Of course, you don't realize it then. You're just a kid. You think that this is just life, and it's normal, until you realize it's not. It's when you're older and you think, "What the…?"

This all has to do with "Perception is Reality." How you perceive something when you're five or ten years old is completely different from how you'll perceive it when you're twenty or thirty. How you interpret a movie, experience, or book, is also based on perception. It's based on what has determined your perception (for example, childhood trauma, social activities, interactions, events experiences, family upbringing, what you had for dinner, how much sun you got, or if your shoes were tied too tight).Yes, I get it. There are reasons and excuses and justifications for every freaking thing in life. And sometimes (probably most of the time) people use that to their advantage and to the extreme when it's not even applicable, when it has absolutely nothing to do with it. We use these excuses to stay where we are − small and feeling no obligation to do anything else.

## Journal Entry 2016

I'm in beautiful Montana and want to keep this positive, but there are too many clouds. Well actually, it is just one big white puffball that covers the blue sky just above it. It resembles the color gray, which is my least favorite, but still I'm thankful to be here sitting up high on the back deck of Sherry's landlord's home which overlooks the Lake. I spent twenty-four hours here with her nonstop talking, sharing, and it's been truly amazing. I slept in longer than I should have but feel so incredibly rested. I woke up immediately with the thought of Justin saying, "I just miss Amber" when he spoke last night of going on nine dates, only to be disappointed, let down, and believing his true love, the one who has made the stakes too high for anyone else to compete with, is the only one he wants.

And I got it. That is exactly what happens when you try to move on after a recent break up. OK, loss. There is no way anyone will measure up to the expectations, that which once were all the things you loved about them—their cute little quirks, mannerisms, facial expressions. The way their lips move when they speak. Their laugh, the way they walk. The eyes- the window to the soul if one let you. The television shows, music, and all the conversations you shared. Yes, it's all completely different and feels so foreign, and it only leaves you missing that person more. Stop dating. You're going to think and remember it was so much better than it really was. Seriously, it wasn't. It's just that the movie playing in your mind, the so-called memories, is so convincing when the lighting is so perfect and the music is playing in the background, stirring up all the emotions of a beautiful and well-thought-out love story. You have no choice but to sit back and watch and feel what the executive producers have so carefully created. You are a captive audience. Stand up and walk out of the theater! It's fiction, and like any Award-winning movie producer and production, it was designed to pull you in and make you believe.

So, what can you believe in today?

*Our Lives are not determined by what happens to us but how we react to what happens, not by what life brings to us but by our attitude we bring to life.*

## Life, Death, and The Rope

There is life after death, real or perceived. Yes, you've gone through something terrible, and sometimes, it feels like you're the only one. Whatever it is that I thought: shame, embarrassment, humiliation, feeling like you can't face anything anymore. I know how it feels to feel alone and like an outcast, to be stripped from what you've known and loved for so long, from your identity, your purpose, and reason for the day ahead, wondering what you should do now. Where do you even begin? How do you even start to pick up the pieces and move on? Move on with your next phase of life, a new you with more wisdom and understanding?

You can, even though right now it feels and seems impossible. Right now, you can't see or even imagine anything different than what your life used to be before you were publicly humiliated, before your world crumbled all around you like dominos or building blocks falling over. It's going to take faith and a new willingness to allow something else. A new life is waiting for you if you only believe.

I love the story "The Rope." The story tells about a mountain climber who wanted to climb the highest mountain. He began his adventure after many years of preparation, but since he wanted the glory just for himself, he decided to climb the mountain alone. He started to climb, but it began to get very late, and instead of preparing his tent to camp, he kept climbing. It got very dark.

As he was climbing, only a few feet away from the top of the mountain, he slipped and fell into the air at a great speed. The climber could only see black spots as he went down and the terrible sensation of being sucked by gravity. He kept falling and in those moments of great fear, it came to his mind, all the good and bad episodes of his life. He was thinking now about how close death was getting when all of a sudden, he felt the rope tied to his waist pull him very hard. His body was hanging in the air. Only the rope was holding him, and in that moment of stillness, he had no other choice but to scream, "Help me, God!"

All of a sudden, a deep voice coming from the sky answered, "What do you want me to do?"

"Save me, God!"

"Do you really think I can save you?"

"Of course, I believe you can."

"Then cut the rope tied to your waist."

There was a moment of silence, and the man decided to hold on to the rope with all his strength. The rescue team tells that the very next day, a climber was found dead and frozen, his body hanging from a rope, his hands holding tight to it only ten feet away from the ground.

And you? How attached are you to your rope? Will you let go?

Trust and have faith.

# Chapter 9:

# Persevere

I always thought and felt I knew who I was, feeling like a rock on a solid foundation. I knew with all my being I was doing God's work, the work of the universe, and I would always be empowered because it was truth and for the good of all. I felt one hundred percent safe and secure knowing God knew my heart and true intentions with everything I did and every word that I spoke. I felt completely protected, feeling like I had a shield around me that no one or bad thing could penetrate. It was a misconception that slapped me in the face when everything came crashing down.

How could that be? Wasn't I living a truthful, and righteous (term used loosely) life? I had scripture on the walls of my beautiful office, confessing my faith publicly, did everything right and honest, knowing everything is seen, even though most isn't in the world. It was important for me to live a life that was pure in the sight of god. After all, I felt completely blessed with all that I had and continued to accomplish because I thought I was being blessed with the way I was living, so was I now being punished?

Everything was happening so fast. It was like a whirlwind, and I was so humbled with what I felt God was entrusting me with - people, clients, employees, relationships, being able to truly help witness to and make an impact on their lives forever. Who would have thought what once made me feel so fulfilled, now leaves me devastated beyond what I think is even repairable in this lifetime. How do I live with all of that?

There's nothing I wanted more than to feel like I was living a life that mattered...that I was born and meant to fulfill. I've always wanted to be an A+ student, good little girl, and to make my mom proud. I don't think there's any preparation for hitting rock bottom, especially when you can't even imagine what that would be like in the first place. Holy mackerel - having to live through your worst nightmare is something that will stay with you forever. How can it not?

So funny (not really) how you think you've got it all figured out—goals and plans in place, feeling calculated, on top of it all and carrying it all out in physical form and with precision details. It's actually hilarious if you really think about it - like we're all that. Everything we thought...the accomplishing our desires and that we controlled it all.

## Map Out and Visualize Your New Destination

Yes, we can dream, plan, set goals, learn, anticipate, and put it all into action, but in the end, stuff happens and maybe because it's about something other than ourselves. Life isn't as simplistic as we think it is, running linear lines with guaranteed outcomes. We're all connected by invisible thread together as one large unit, one world, family, body coexisting in this world, not to mention the most powerful unseen world of spirit, the source of all life that most can't even comprehend because they were taught to operate only from the five senses. If you can't see it, it's not real. If it's not backed up and proven scientifically, it doesn't count.

We distrust our total gut instinct and intuition because we're always looking for outside validation, questioning ourselves versus the people trying to convince us otherwise. When you grow up seeking approval from others in authority (OK, well from whoever), you're receptive to explanations, dialog, reasoning, and so-called facts instead of listening to our own voice.

For me, I just wanted to feel certain, to believe in someone, something, and to be completely committed and convicted, knowing what I stood up for. It's what empowered me, made me feel alive, and that was all mattered. It's worthless and hard to live without purpose, passion, and meaning; otherwise, you're just going through the motions.

The good news is that when you do hit rock bottom, the thing you could never even imagine, there's nowhere else to go but up. Yay. It's also the perfect foundation to build your new identity in life future career, so that's exciting, right?

But wait, that means I need to do something other than wallow in my misery and what happened. And then, I'll have to set new goals and plans, and what if it doesn't work out again?

Oh my gosh, I don't even know if I have the energy to do it all over again. Especially without all of the optimistic confidence (real or imagined, it's the same) that I used to have. All I have to work off of, is my past failure and disgrace and the memory of it. How am I supposed to keep myself positive and motivated, with great expectations, when I cringe just thinking about stepping outside my house? Seriously.

How am I supposed to handle rejection, conflict, hold and carry myself in a manner worthy of clients, let alone earning their trust as well as just trusting myself?

I'm exhausted, and I'm still in my bathrobe.

It's important to start with where you are. Write it all down. Yes, it may be miscalculated, over-exaggerated, better or worse off than you thought, but perception is reality, so it is important to get it all out so you can move on from here/there in order to get a fresh start.

## Understanding the Journey along the Way

It's a healing process that takes time. For me, I was so used to setting my mind on something, a goal to do, or an accomplishment and I would just do it. I knew the steps, what I had to do to accomplish them, which ultimately resulted in the end product and price. Frankly, it was easy. As long as you were willing to put in the time, effort, and work, it was obtainable, achievable and basically inevitable when you followed the plan and strategy you laid out.

Healing, on the other hand, is not like just picking up the rake to accomplish filling the yard waste cans to put out on the curb side before morning. It's not doing twenty minutes of cardio on the treadmill or making the ten phone calls before 5:00 p.m., going to the store, cleaning out the fridge or litter box. Having sex, painting the walls, giving the dog a bath, baking a cake, making the bed, pulling weeds, washing the car, scrubbing the floors, doing windows, shaving your legs, sorting out the junk drawer, dropping off good-will bags and picking up your kids on the way back, and don't even get me started on the 1,000 things to do in the attic. You get the picture. My point is healing is hard and takes time, along with a lot of emotional work, which is a million times harder than any physical labor or task.

Being able to gauge and assess how far you've come is easy when it's about whether or not the dishwasher has been unloaded. It's obvious. Task completed. Check. Move on. But in personal, unseen work, one day you feel you've made progress with healing the wounded adult, forgiving past circumstances, cradling the little child within, rewarding yourself for being strong, and voicing your true feelings out loud, expressing your needs on paper, reading two pages of your favorite Tony Robbins book, believing you've already implemented one of the life-changing strategies that really is going to make the difference...but

## It's Never a Straight Path

*Wait, what?*

All of a sudden, I'm back to square one, in fetal position, on the bathroom floor, the one that wasn't scrubbed clean.

*Seriously? I thought I was totally making progress! I really thought I was finally moving on from the past*

*and moving forward with the new future! What just happened?!? I'm just going to go to bed and start all over again tomorrow. Hopefully, I'll feel better and see things differently. Good night.*

The problem is, it's not just tomorrow. Its day after day. You tell yourself differently, but it's not. Suddenly, it all blends in with the same excuse: there's always tomorrow. But then you realize it hasn't been. You've stopped shaving your legs and now everyone mistakes you for Chewbacca, and your fruits and vegetables are molded in a position unrecognizable in the bottom of the crisper drawer in the fridge.

Year after year, you continue to make excuses.

You know what? It doesn't really matter. I have time; after all, I have gone through so much. Nobody expects anything other than what I'm doing, right? I've accomplished so much more than most have up to this point. Besides, it doesn't really matter. And beyond that…

*Stop. You're kidding? It has not been over a decade! Has it?*

Wow, you're right. The kids have graduated. My niece now has two children I never even met, and people I've known all of a sudden look like an animated character with aging-producing effects for a new movie. I don't even recognize them.

Holy mackerel, everyone is and has moved on, and I'm still here stuck back in 2006, moping around like I have the right to.

Who am I? And where do I even start? If I am not my image, identity, career, monetary worth, title, status, then who am I? Easier said than done. Trust me, I know. I thought I knew, but truthfully, it's easy to stand up and make a noise when people see you in a way that gives you authority and respect... when you feel worthy enough to speak up.

I'm not sure where you are in your business field, chosen career path, or life, but I do know if you picked up this book, there is a reason.

I wrote this for you. And I'd love to save you all the time and pain of being lost, feeling ashamed and humiliated, and not knowing what to do. I've had over thirteen torturous years dealing suffering, settling, excuses, negotiations, inner and outer dialog, nonstop, hiding, fear, uncertainty, unresolved pain and forgiveness, answers, lack of living short of potential and trying to be OK with it.

Chapter 10:

# Surrender

*Be Still and Know*
*—Psalms 46:10, New International Version*

*Do what you were called to do*
*Showing up is the first step and to persevere is*
*showing your strength, character, and courage.*

Y ou got to be thankful! Seriously, it all starts with having something to look forward to. Dr. Wayne Dyer writes in all his books (which by the way, I have most of them) that the first thing that you need to do when opening your eyes, is to be thankful. Be thankful and express being thankful. Sometimes it's hard though, right? I mean, he doesn't know what we went through. How can you be all happy and optimistic when my life is falling apart?

But the fact of the matter is, when you do sit and think first thing in the morning, *what* you are thankful, not *if* you are thankful; it makes a huge difference. It puts your heart and mind in the right place and the right perspective. It sets the whole day up, with circumvents that continues to trickle into the rest of the day. Every day, I journal. Sometimes its short and simple, just with the date, day, and time, along with the song in my head that I woke up to (I can count on my hand how many days that I *didn't* have one. To me, its special, and I know there is a hidden meaning or message), and then I write out at least five things I'm thankful for. Some days, it's challenging and it may only state things like, thank you for the beautiful blue sky and the sun shining bright, the birds I hear chirping happily, the phone calls and emails I accomplished yesterday even though it was busy and full, my full tank of gas, leftovers so I don't have to cook. You get the picture. There is *always* something. And then other times, I can literally write for hours. Poetry flows through me as fast as I can write. I have included some of these as well, in addition some of my other affirmations that you definitely need to get in the habit of doing. Again, huge difference!

Today I woke up with total love in my heart. Thank you for my suddenly different perspective on so many things. For opening my heart and mind to see a new picture, imagine, a new life and what is real and has been all along—in front and inside me. For the relationship that I have in my heart and soul for Tammy, Tom's sister. For Susie, though I am still sad she never got to experience a different human life experience, searching for so many years, in order to live the life acceptable to Jehovah, which meant sacrificing everything, including her own family. I am thankful she shared her life with me. I totally believe she actually saved it. I do feel loss of the opportunity to get to know Tammy, though I learned so much from Tom in the beginning. Her hanging swing/hammock, her belief in God and the divine world. Finally getting to visit her home at the time of her death. To scan her book shelves where I saw Mitch Albom's book I love so much, *For One More Day,* and the scriptures I carry deep in my heart and visibly in my own home. *Be still and know. With God all things are possible.* Thank you for the transformation I sense in Taylor and the consistency of our long-distance relationship.

I finally feel like I get to be the helpful and guiding mother he still needs at the age of twenty-four years old...like I'm watching him grow up. I can still see a new vision of what he's becoming. Tom's sweet demeanor and the love I feel for him, looking at his innocence through his anger. My CD, "Healing Waters." The writers workshop. Plants and birds that fly free outside of a cage. My books. Thomas's hugs. Baelee's personality, which consistently makes me seriously laughed my butt off so hard and out loud.

## Surrender

We are the change, the seeds of the future, and we determine it with what we give out both in thought and deed. The future is now. We are more powerful each and every single one of us then we even know or comprehend. It only takes one person, one word, one act of kindness that can literally change the course of history. Most of the time, we don't really believe we make a difference, but all of us united contribute to the compound effect that creates the world we live in and draws the map of tomorrow.

I believe there is no better exercise for the heart than reaching out and lifting others up.

Chapter 11:

# Letters

## Letters to Loved Ones

**G**oing through any trial or tribulation shows you so much about yourself and others. The majority of the experience has been painful, but it is such a complete blessing to be able to see the hearts of those who are dedicated to stand by you. It's those few people that make all the difference, sometimes the difference between life and death. I am thankful for the few sincere and committed people who have helped me through the darkest and scariest time of my life.

## Letter to Thomas, my ex-husband (October 9, 2014) and still stands true to this day.

The longer I travel this life, the more I know there

is not many things or people who are exactly what they seem or start out to be. This conclusion has been a painful experience and a lesson I've not been fond of and still want to reject. However, the one thing I do know for sure, the thing that has not changed or wavered is your true character and your core genetic makeup that defines the authentic and pure person you are.

Just when I lose hope in all humanity, you shine through, reminding me there is still a glimmer of hope, a hope to believe in another, in one's motive and real self. After everything and all the years in between (the almighty only knows), you continue to show me that you are the same and stand true, not only to who you are and portray to be, but more.

I am delighted and in awe of your raw and forthcoming affection that dwells deep within your heart, and the fact that, without false barriers for facades, you humbly acknowledge and reveal inside what could so easily be misunderstood or somehow used against you. You are and have continued to express your open vulnerability in being so kind and loving toward me. Me. Your ex-wife. Your supposed enemy.

Where jealousy and rage could easily breed, you sow only love. I am so forever thankful, Thomas, that you are the father of our children and that we have the relationship that we do. You have been nothing but completely consistent with upholding values that most don't and can't even comprehend. Remember talking about Bruce Willis and Demi Moore? That their relationship resembled ours? Why does it have to be so hard, awkward, or hateful? I am so thankful we chose to raise our children together with love and knowing that their future is dependent upon what they see, witness, experience, and the love that the mom and dad have for each other.

The love, dedication, and support you have for your children is seriously unimaginable and in which no role model exists. I am just lucky that you overflow with so much to give and that I get to participate in the receiving. You have been such an incredible example of unconditional love and a witness at the highest level. To truly evaluate, realize, and conclude, you need to be able to reflect and ponder. I am doing that tonight, thinking of you, and knowing how extremely blessed I am.

Thank you for giving me more than I deserve. And mostly, for showing me that through everything, when you could have done so much to hurt me (if it was even in you), you chose and continue to look at and believe in the good of others. Thank you for letting one of them be me. I will love you always.

## Letter From My Daughter

This letter is exactly why I'm alive today. It was from my daughter on Mother's Day just couple years ago, and with her still being a teenager. I know I am beyond lucky, beyond the expression of blessed. I know, and its exactly why I live today.

"Wow. By society's standards, you finally get the recognition you deserve for all the hard work and contributions you give during the year, although you and I both would argue that's something we should celebrate each and every day. Happy Mother's Day mama. Without you, I would wouldn't be here in life... literally. *crowd gives half-hearted chuckle* On a deeper note, man, I am so glad and blessed to have my twin and greatest role model be the woman that I am not only related to, but live with and get to wake up with mediocre cups of coffee and silly "rise and shine" songs. I will forever feel that my life is advantageous over any others for the simple reason that I was born in the hands of you − a presence on this Earth that is so rare and limited, a type of extraordinary that is inconceivable. I know God, the Universe, whatever you want to call it, took extra time to etch your face and body to the fantasy-like qualities that you are, to give you the purest form of empathy and grace and provide you with the greatest intrinsic authenticity, realness, and charm. You are the only human being that I can transparently look at, as if you are made of glass and that I could see your actual beating heart pumping hard, and your veins and cells all working together to keep you alive. I see you for you and there is no bad... no flaws or imperfections. It's weird. I guess that's proof of just how deeply I love you. Thank you mom, for setting the standards in which I aspired to be. You do such an amazing job at making sure I feel absolutely loved and secure, you never have to question or doubt whether I feel it. You juggle and balance maintaining a life of your own on top of providing for the lives around you and your selflessness never goes unnoticed. I want to imitate everything about you, and that's always been a part of me. Even when I couldn't comprehend the massive successes you've had and the adversities that you've overcome. I still remember and can see myself when I was little, watching you get ready in the bathroom. Leaning over the counter on your tippy toes to be closer to the mirror, perfecting the last touches of make up on your face with your hair up in rollers. You are naked and rushing. I remember analyzing you and thinking of you in the highest, highest regards. I thought that you are superwoman! And not for anything that you did or gave me, literally just for being you. That image of you being superwoman in my head has only gotten clearer and stronger the older I get. You are the epitome of ideal beauty and spirit and someone worth fighting to be like every day of my life. I'm sorry for not verbalizing it more because you deserve to be reminded of just how extraordinary you are each and every day. I am so lucky and grateful to live my best life beside you, my Mini me. I mean, thank God there's at least one person in my life that "gets me," am I right? You know that saying goes I be lost without you? Yeah I would feel like life was one big twiddle my thumbs playground without you in it. Here I am striking it rich every day with you. You add the greatest worth to my life mom. I love you. Your Daughter, Baelee"

## Letter from Me to Myself

I wrote this to my Ego in the form and from the perspective of wanting to reengage and connect to myself, to deepen the bond after years of trying to connect and with the conflicting side we all have unconsciously, the part of us that controls more than we even know or want to admit. Acknowledging and coming to terms with this conflicting and defiant part of us is the first step in moving forward and facing our fears. It sheds light in the areas we've been too afraid to go, calling out and confronting the demons, actually exposes their lack of power and hold over us. By stepping up, facing our fears head-on, they dissolve, and we're finally free from the constant background noise and to live and be who we really are. Fully vulnerable. Fully alive. This is for us. A heartfelt letter for you and I.

I said I would always be real with you. I liked that I allowed myself to truly open up for the first time ever, to be honest and vulnerable with you because I trusted you loved me for who I really was and not just an image of who you thought or wanted me to be.

For the first time, I wasn't afraid. I dropped my walls, and I let you in. For the first time, I was completely confident and knew deep in my core that you really, really loved me. Even at my darkest hour with being incarcerated without communication, I felt certain you were there. You fought for us from the very beginning. Through all the obstacles and what seemed impossible, we didn't give up. You didn't give up, even when I felt I wanted to.

I want to go back to that place, that place of undeniable love and knowing we are supposed to be together. We were destined, and now we are blessed.

I recently looked at all the pictures of us that surround my mom's room, and we were so happy. Our faces glowed with obvious love and affection for each other. We were assertive in being together without any hindrance of where we were or who we were with, including my ex-husband in his home.

I love you with all my heart. I just want us to go back, for you to go back to the positive attitude of knowing there is nothing impossible in finding solutions to the everyday obstacles and frustrations of life. And me with loving you without guarded reservation. I want to change the negative association and all the defense mechanisms I have when talking with you, the hard shell I've surrounded myself with because I know you're disappointed with me/us and our current life-style and irritations. I want to live in total harmony no matter what the day brings, to live fully in the present moment every hour.

I don't want to "test" you to see if you still want us or if it means something when you don't hold my hand or snuggle me on the couch. I don't want to be sad when we see each other and don't hug anymore or that we say I love you out of habit and without intention. I don't want to feel as though I can't do anything right or meet your expectations when I feel I am working harder than I ever have.

I want to see the love in your eyes when you look at me. I want to hear the smile in your voice when we talk and look forward to when you call. I want to feel that you want us/me with all your heart and not just because we live together and this is our life now. I want to discard all of the negative neuro-associations that have crept into our relationship.

I don't want to get to the point of thinking about our relationship ending and feeling the pain of separation before we realize this is what we want and are willing to change. I don't want to imagine being without you or thinking of plan B and start numbing myself so I can deal with it. I love you more than anything. I should be willing to do anything for you. I need to know you're willing to do the same for me. I promise to be more balanced with a regular routine if you promise to be a little more open, light-hearted, and spontaneous.

I want you to remember how I could do no wrong in your eyes, when you stuck up for me even when I didn't for myself, seeing the innocence in me like you used to, completely and unconditionally.

I want our beautiful love story to continue to grow and unfold into a best-selling novel, an example of what love really is. I want my kids/your kids that you are helping to raise to look up to our relationship and know what love really is, the way it should be, and what they would expect it to be when looking for their spouse and the love of their life.

I want to know that true love does exist and that it is possible for me when I never thought it was. I want to hold in my heart how I've never felt this way before and bring back to life the miracle I witnessed being able to live a life with you after all those years and obstacles between us. I truly believe we were brought together through divine intervention and what we have is a gift.

I believe that we both want the same thing. It just seems like it's difficult for us to live and express it now in our daily lives. So, what can I do to bring out the best in you? To empower you to be the being you are and continue to want to be? What can I do to help us get on track and really live the life we've always dreamt about? You say that it's really just you, but really, it's us, and it's up to us to change our reality to reflect our truest and highest self. It's not just you anymore. You are no longer living solo. It's we now, and we can change anything we want. Do you want to?

I don't want the daily routine and business of life to automatically program our existence, to just run off default. I want to purposely navigate our journey in the direction that we know will lead us to our exact destination. We know how to do this. We accomplished huge goals independently.

Surely, we can set up some new ones and succeed in them as well together. There are two of us now, so it should be easier if we build each other up and work together as one, the one we should be anyway, right?

Come on. Regardless of what it is, we can kick butt, so let's just do it. Let's take our list set our minds and put it into action, one step at a time, just as you've told me before to do on so many occasions. Look at how you have helped me go through the most frightening and hardest period of my life. Even through the dark and scary unknown and all of the uncertainty of being completely out of control, I/we survived.

I'm sure that you could list just one or two things that would make a huge difference. Let's start with them and move forward. Pretty soon, we'll have days, then weeks of living differently, and that will only motivate us to do a few more. We are not completely happy because we know we are not living up to our full potential, a standard we know in our heart. We are way too young and have way more drive than to live with mediocrity. As I write this, I am motivating myself to start doing what I keep thinking about doing.

I love you honey, and I'm hoping I was able to express myself without any misunderstanding as to my true intention for us. Please know that I want to hear your thoughts and feedback (as long as you're nice about it), and I know it didn't include everything we could talk about, especially your point of view. It's only Tuesday, so let's make the best of the rest of the week while we still have some alone quiet time.

## Journal of Dream

"Can someone just hold me, don't fix me, don't try to change a thing. I'm broken, and it's beautiful (Kelly Clarkson). I woke up this morning speaking out loud confidently and assertively. Angela was stuck in Chicago, Illinois and left me a message asking me to cover her this morning at the board of realtors meeting for about forty-five minutes and put in a good plug for her since she wouldn't be able to make it. She ended by saying you don't have to, but if you do or you don't, you'll never be the same. I knew what she meant. I knew she was testing me. She knew I had so much inside that I kept holding on to and if I could just release it get over it once and for all for real not just talk about it, it would change me forever. I knew I blew it when I was there in D.C. and met her for the first time at the three-day live event and training. I was an emotional wreck. She said, "Leesa, your IQ is off the charts, and I know you could sell and do anything, but it's *you* who's holding you back, and you've got to work on what's inside and feel worthy." She was right. I've known for years that I was stopping everything in my life because of being afraid, the constant self-dialogue that ran through my mind at all times, reminding me of what a screw up I was, reliving and replaying the events that led up to my breakdown, but more important than that, just the horror of everything, the people I hurt, the embarrassment and shame and public humiliation I felt and still feel every single day. There's still so much I don't and can't remember. Like it's one big foggy dream or nightmare with no beginning and no end. I was just in the middle of this chaos trying to figure out what the heck was going on, spinning in circles, dizzy with confusion, not believing what was happening all around me like some world catastrophe where every-one is running around in all directions with no organization, everyone just on their own trying to find their loved ones and run to safety.

I just knew I had to do what Angela asked even though I was scared and had less than forty-five minutes to get showered and ready while trying to think about my opening line in front of all my old peers and colleagues. I didn't have time to prepare for any of it, and maybe that was a good thing—not enough time to freak out and worry myself right out of doing it. Man, she's so smart, and I was thinking, she cared enough to want to stretch me and pushed my limits instead of allowing me off the hook and continue to use my past as an excuse to stay exactly where I've been for over a decade. Comfortable, but not comfortable. How can wallowing in misery in the past, in something I can never, ever change no matter how bad I felt, no matter how much I wanted it to be different. It never would be. I can't go back. I can't redo anything. But I can change now. What I think what I am doing, my current present, my future. I told Maria not to talk to me because I needed to concentrate on getting ready and think about what I was going to say.

I kept thinking about what I thought Angela would want me to say about her company like a sales pitch. What would make her proud? What was she hoping for? I envisioned her also being there in the back watching with a smile, knowing I stepped up to the plate, that I was doing the absolute thing I've been running and hiding from for so many years. No baby steps. No dipping your toe in the pool to see if it was cold. No. Just jumping in and feeling this slow motion, knowing you're going to hit the water, submerge, shocked at the cold and the deafness underneath until you swim up to the surface and breathe air. Exhilarating. I just did it without over thinking. I just jumped in, and it was incredible! I'm thankful I took the plunge, that I just did it. Thinking about Angela and not myself for once, made all the difference, not only because I felt like I lost my opportunity to show her who I really was verses this Over emotional, week crybaby, playing the same old song-and-dance, like somehow I would be excused because of all the bad things that have happened to me, like somehow my stuff was so much worse than anyone else's.

She didn't break. She didn't console me with tears in her eyes telling me she "understands," and it's OK, She doesn't blame me for feeling the way I do and tells me she didn't even know how I got there and through it all. "Put all of that trauma on top of your childhood—wow! You definitely have a reason to be sad and give up. Yes, Leesa, of course you have the right to feel the way you do. You're strong just because you're living. You went through all of that and didn't commit suicide like so many others have over lesser things. You stuck it out, and you deserve to stay stuck and play the victim. You poor thing." No, she wasn't having it. She was not going to give in or allow me the reasoning of being depressed and feeling like I'll never be able to get over it this—not that she was mean or anything. I knew she cared and felt her sincerity. She was on the other side, steadfast, holding my hands, pulling me out of the quicksand. But the more I resisted and struggled, the faster I sunk. It was only when I stopped resisting, when I took a deep breath and just surrendered, I was totally and finally pulled to the shore. What I thought was impossible, when I couldn't even see a way out and felt hopeless, I was now free, safe and out of danger. I did it, and here I am, so thankful she didn't give up even when I wanted to.

But she couldn't do it forever. She couldn't want it more than I did for myself. "It's either a heck yes or a hard no, but make up your mind already. You've been in limbo for way too long, so if it's not now, when?" She was right; when would it all change? When I did. It was up to me to move forward and realized I was wasting time, my life, the thing that's gone forever. I was using my now-thinking and regretting the past.

I think for so many of us we forget our time here on earth is limited. We think there's always tomorrow. Yep, another day. Another day another dollar as we drag ourselves out of bed dreading the workday ahead.

We take it for granted that we only have now, this very moment. Nothing else is guaranteed. Take the gift.

## Do You Remember? A Journal Entry to myself June 27th, 2011

I wrote this when I thought I was waking up, when I thought I was going to start moving forward. It wasn't for another seven years or so that I finally *remembered*.

Do you remember how you used to dream before all life's disappointments, before you were let down, betrayed, rejected, and hurt?

Do you remember how easy it used to be? To wake up with total excitement for the day and all the possibilities? To have so much enthusiasm bursting forth you thought you would explode?

Do you remember how you thought there was absolutely nothing you could not do? And how this assured confidence seeped through every pore of your being, and you just knew without question or hesitation, that today awaited something incredibly miraculous, and all you had to do was be awake and receive and witness it unfold before your very eyes?

Do you remember what it was like knowing that all things were possible and experiencing the joy, the happiness and total bliss, of creating the life you've always imagined and more?

To be living a dream in the present moment and helping others believe and live it to?

Remember how empowered you felt? And how your light shined and illuminated from your very core that it showered on everyone you came in contact with? A light so pure, so bright, you glowed undeniably regardless of your surroundings?

Do you remember how bold you were and passionate? Your presence was magnetic and contagious and your radiance a shield that surrounded you.

Do you remember how you purposely looked into another's eyes, loving the connection you had with another, and a smile, a warm embrace is the best gift to anyone? Making others feel important? Utilizing your gifts and position to help others, not for you to be in the spotlight but for them?

Do you remember all the laughter throughout the day that burst through almost every conversation? And that to act and be too serious was just stupid?

Do you remember how you sang and danced no matter where you were?

Do you remember who you are?

The real you? Authentic and full of love and power?

Let your light shine again. Be the force, the instrument, the pure being of total abundance you are designed to be, that you know you are, full of purpose, passion, and driving determination. Be the hope and example that others so desperately need.

Lead the way again.

Stand up.

Step out.

Wake up, Leesa.

Be born again, and remember who you are.

Just remember.

# Acknowledgments

There are so many people that I can't even begin to acknowledge or thank for standing by me through the most difficult time. I wouldn't be here if it weren't for my brother David and my sister in law Agnes, who while living in Panama came out to California several times to be with me and to make sure I was ok, as well as taking care of our mother financially, who was suffering with Alzheimer's in a residential facility.

And to Tom, who has been my strength when I couldn't think of any value or purpose in myself, in addition to spending an enormous amount of money, time, and so much more to assist me with my freedom and building me back up emotionally again, for over the past ten years. I would have given up long before.

To my sister Maria and her husband Larry for their forgiveness and unconditional love and the life we continue to share. Thank you for always making me feel so special and welcomed.

My sweet Louie, my private investigator who worked hard from the beginning, on both court convictions and trials for years, assisted me at every court hearing, personally picked me up, and made me feel safe and secure, all in addition to his job of completing research on my behalf. He was my savior. I am forever grateful.

To Erica - my sweet agent, my angel - who risked her own reputation standing up for me, going around and getting testimonies, speaking for me on my behalf when I didn't have a voice, and believing in me more than anyone. You were my biggest cheerleader. I love you so much.

To Angela, for creating such a beautiful and thorough platform for others to share their message and providing everything needed to do so. And to Emily — you are so amazing, a beautiful light and such a loving heart throughout this overwhelming process. Your patience and grace are so appreciated more than mere words can articulate. You believed in me when I didn't for myself. I absolutely would not have been able to complete this book without you!

For Michael, who adores me more than I deserve and allowed me to "work," a.k.a. hang out, at his store The Postal Annex, so I could socialize and interact with his customers and give extra tight hugs, allowing me to feel the joy I once knew and crave. He was so instrumental to my healing.

And to my children Baelee, Thomas, and Taylor, who love me so much, more than I could ever ask for. If for no other reason or purpose for my life but to be your mother, I have been completely successful. Thank you for trusting me to take care of you. You are the reason I live.

Thank you to David Hancock and the Morgan James Publishing team for helping me bring this book to print.

# Thank You

Thank you for helping me leave a greater footprint in the world with your willingness, participation, love, and support. We can all do it together, one person at a time, and one day at a time. For those embarking on this journey with me thus far–thank you for trusting me with your heart in reading this book and for wanting to make a change. You deserve it. Afterwards, you will wonder why it took you so long to make this decision.

We only have so much time together in this book and it is only the tip of the iceberg. There is no way I'd be able to articulate everything I hope for you as well as provide all the tools, techniques, and strategies I'd like and want to share. Please email me at leesa.tlc@gmail.com for a free strategy consultation. I'd be more than happy to give you the action workbook I created, that will help you outline your goals and identify what you need to overcome what you're going through, and to get to the next level of your healing. The most important thing, is to take action… starting today. You can obviously do this on your own or we can do this together. Trust me, it's so much easier when you have real support and with a partner, to help guide you, every step of the way. One that has been there, who understands exactly where you are. It is my sincere hope that I have contributed in some way, that has or will change your life. I'd love to hear how you're doing, changes you've made and implemented, and what you have achieved so far. We all help each other.

With sincere love, xoxox

# About the Author

Leesa Ward is now *retired* from the real estate business where she worked from 1987-2006. She has now found the blessing in continuing to do what she's always loved—working with people, one-on-one and helping them grow, move past the pain of shame and achieve their new goals in becoming their real, authentic spirit. Leesa currently lives in southern California and is a proud mother to her three children.